Champion Ozmilion Dedication, born 20 April, 1985 (sire: Ch Ozmilion Admiration, dam: Ch Ozmilion Heart's Desire); Dog World-Pedigree Chum Top Dog of All Breeds 1987 (32 Challenge Certificates, 1 Best in Show and 2 Reserve Best in Show; Toy Group winner at Crufts 1988. Bred and owned by Osman Sameja, Dedication is the tenth generation of home-bred champion Ozmilion dogs in direct tail male.

A DOG OWNER'S GUIDE TO
YORKSHIRE TERRIERS

a Salamander book

Published by Salamander Books Limited
LONDON ● NEW YORK

A DOG OWNER'S GUIDE TO

YORKSHIRE TERRIERS

Jackie Ransom

Photographs by Marc Henrie

A Salamander Book

© Salamander Books
129, 137 York Way,
London N7 9LG

ISBN 0-86101-371-9

Distributed in the UK by Hodder and Stoughton Services, PO Box 6, Mill Road, Dunton Green, Sevenoaks, Kent TN13 2XX.

Credits

Editor: Jo Finnis
Designer: Philip Gorton
Photographs: Marc Henrie
Illustrations: Ray Hutchins
Colour origination: Rodney Howe Ltd
Typesetting: The Old Mill
Printed in Portugal

Contents

Author

Jackie Ransom is a member of the Kennel Club and The Breed Standards And Stud Book Committee in the United Kingdom.
Since her first judging appointment in 1965, Jackie quickly found herself in demand to judge both in the UK and many other countries worldwide. She has judged at Crufts Dog Show several times, and has been passed by the Kennel Club to judge the Toy Group. She also awards Challenge Certificates to breeds in the Working and Utility Groups.
Jackie has also established an enviable record in breeding, showing and judging the Bichon Frisé, and has also bred many top-winning Poodles.
Author of *A Dog Owner's Guide To Standard, Miniature & Toy Poodles*, published by Salamander, Jackie has also written many articles for various magazines worldwide, and has contributed the Breed Notes to *Dog World*, a top-selling dog paper in the UK, since 1974.
Jackie lives in Wembley Park, near London, where she has a splendid library of historical dog publications, cards and prints.

Contributor

Trevor Turner qualified from the Royal Veterinary College, London, in 1958 and within a few months had set up a small animal practice at his home in Northolt, near London. He now runs an extensive small animal hospital employing over 30 people.

Trevor was brought up with Terriers and has always owned dogs and cats in multiplicity. Litters are planned and bred on an occasional basis.

An active member of many veterinary associations and past president of some, Trevor writes and speaks widely on a variety of topics connected with small animal practice. He believes that the role of the vet involves not only treatment of the patient but also intelligible communication with the owners, who should always feel free to question and discuss problems with the veterinarian.

US consultant

Hal Sundstrom, as president of Halamar Inc, publishers of North Virginia, has been editing and publishing magazines on travel and pure-bred dogs since 1972. He is the recipient of six national writing and public excellence awards from the Dog Writer's Association of America, of which he is now president, and he is a past member of the Collie Club of America. He is now a delegate to the American Kennel Club representing the Collie Club.

Hal has an extensive background and enormous experience in the dog world as a breeder/handler/exhibitor, match and sweeps judge, officer and director of specialty and all-breed clubs, show and symposium chairman, and officer of the Arizona and Hawaii Councils of Dog Clubs.

Photographer

Marc Henrie began his career as a Stills Man at the famous Ealing Film Studios in London. He then moved to Hollywood where he worked at MGM, RKO, Paramount and Warner Brothers, photographing the Hollywood greats: Humphrey Bogart, Edward G Robinson, Gary Cooper, Joan Crawford and Ingrid Bergman, to name a few. He was one of the last photographers to photograph Marilyn Monroe.

Later, after he had returned to England, Marc specialized in photographing dogs and cats, rapidly establishing an international reputation.

He has won numerous photographic awards, most recently the Kodak Award for the Best Animal Photograph and the Neal Foundation Award for Outstanding Photography of Animal Behaviour.

Marc is married to ex-ballet dancer, Fiona Henrie, who now writes and illustrates books on animals. They live in West London with their daughter Fleur, two Cavalier King Charles Spaniels and a cat called Topaz.

Author's acknowledgments

The author and editor would like to thank the following people for their invaluable contributions to the book: Osman Sameja for writing the Introduction and helping with photography; R Enze and B Downey (cover shot — Ch Shantmarles President of Yat, owned by R Enze and B Downey), Patsy Bloom and Brian Johns of Petcetera Etc for helping with photography; John and Margaret Wells, Keriwell Yorkshire Terriers, for their help with puppy and pet Yorkshire Terrier photographs and captions; The Kennel Club for kind permission to reproduce the Breed Standard, and Gordon Davies, Manager of the Awards Department; Marjorie Ransom for typing the manuscript; Jackie Peace for proof-reading.

Foreword

Osman A Sameja, breeder of international renown; owner/breeder of 30 British Champions

Since the foundation of the breed, the popularity of the Yorkshire Terrier has increased at an enormous rate, making him one of the most sort after dogs of this century.

This man-made animal, although small in size, has a very big heart making him an ideal pet for the whole family. On the other hand, for the fancier who wishes to compete in the show ring, the Yorkshire Terrier is one of the most glamorous breeds of dog.

I have owned and bred these little imps for many years, and for me there can be no other breed. The tenacity of this little dog endears him to all who come into contact with him. He is loyal, loving and a

born show-off. His size makes him an ideal choice for country and urban living alike; he is able to exercise himself in confined areas, yet capable of walking for miles.

The following chapters I found to be factual, informative and interesting. Anyone who wishes to own a Yorkshire Terrier as a pet will find this book helpful, giving clear guidance on what to look for when purchasing a puppy and how to care for him as he grows. It also gives clear advice for the fancier who wishes to enter the world of showing these spectacular little dogs: how to grow the coat as well as an insight into all the paraphernalia so necessary to achieve the glamour of the show specimen.

In conclusion I hope you derive as much pleasure from reading this book as I have.

Chapter One

A HISTORY

Origins
Pillars of the breed
The USA

ORIGINS

The Yorkshire Terrier's ancestors were certainly larger dogs. Huddersfield Ben, as seen and recorded by Gordon Staples in *Our Friend The Dog*, 1883, weighed 12lbs (5.5kg). Today, the Yorkshire Terrier may, according to both the Kennel Club standard in the UK and the American Kennel Club standard, weigh up to 7lbs (3.2kg) only.

In researching the breed's history it is always difficult, when reading old books and articles, to know whether the writer is describing what he or she actually saw or simply repeating what had been written in other books available at the time. However, in *Stonehenge* (second edition dated 1872, England) the following very explicit paragraph appears:

'The Yorkshire Blue Tan, silky-coated Terrier, is a modern breed altogether, having been almost unknown beyond the neighbourhood of Halifax until within the last few years. Excepting in colour and coat this dog resembles the old English rough terrier, as well as the Scotch, but the silky texture of his coat and his rich blue tan are the result of careful selection and probably of crossing with the Maltese. The ears are generally cropped, but if entire should be fine, thin, and moderately small. The coat should be long, silky in texture, and well-parted down the back. The beard is peculiarly long and falling, being often several inches in length, and of a rich golden tan colour. The colour must be entirely blue on the back and down to the elbows and thighs, without any mixture of tan or fawn. The legs and muzzle should be a rich golden tan; the ears being the same, but of a darker shade. On the top of the skull it becomes lighter and almost fawn. The weight varies from 10lbs to 18lbs, *(4.5-8.2kg)*.

PILLARS OF THE BREED

Rawson B Lee, in his book of Terriers published 1894, provides another extract of interest:

'The late Peter Eden of Manchester, so noted in his day for Pugs and Bulldogs, owned Albert, a particularly good Yorkie. Albert had natural drop-ears, and with this variety ear-cropping has increased and may now be said to be general. The Yorkie as a rule has his ears cut, and it is many years since I saw a really first-rate dog on the bench which had not been so mutilated. At the earlier shows excellent specimens appeared with

Below: *Skye Terriers of 1890, thought to be in the ancestry of the Yorkshire Terrier. Note both the pricked and dropped ears.*

their ears entire, and for them special classes were provided.

'Actual measurements go for not very much, but length of the hair on the body and head of some of the best dogs is almost incredible, and its texture and colour are simply extraordinary. It is said that, when in his best form, the little dog Conqueror, owned by Mrs Troughear of Leeds, had hair of almost uniform length of 24 inches *(61cm)*; he weighed about 5½ lbs *(2.5kg)*. One of the smartest little dogs of the variety, and a game little chap, was Mr Kirby's Smart,

Above: *A delightful painting of Mrs M A Foster's Toy Smart, a top show-winning Yorkshire Terrier in England in the year 1879.*

who did a lot of winning about 20 years ago. Old Huddersfield Ben was another of the "pillars of the breed"; Mrs Troughear's Dreadnought was another celebrity; Mrs Foster's Bradford Bright and Sandy were notable dogs a few years ago. To the latter (one of our few lady judges) and her husband, Mr Jonas Foster, more than to anyone else is due any little popularity the Yorkie possesses today. They have bred them for years and have from time to time owned the most perfect specimens imaginable. Mrs Foster's Ted, who

Below: *Taken from the front cover of* Our Dogs *published in England, 1896, the prize-winning Ashton Bright owned by Mrs B M Rice.*

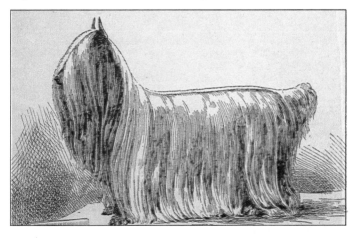

THE
CANINE WORLD
AND SPORTS & SPORTSMEN.

Vol. 1.—No. 13.   FRIDAY, AUG. 15, 1890.   REGISTERED AS A NEWSPAPER AND FOR TRANSMISSION ABROAD   PRICE TWOPENCE.

The Yorkshire Terrier, CHAMPION "TED," (K.C.S.B., 23642).
The property of Mrs. M. A. FOSTER.

weighed 5lbs *(2.3kg)*, perhaps for all-round excellence never was excelled, and it was extremely funny to see this little whippet of a dog competing against an enormous St Bernard or dignified Bloodhound for the cup for the Best Animal in the Show. Nor did the award always go to the big and the strong. One of the tiniest dogs was one of Mrs Foster's, shown at Westminster Aquarium in 1893, Mite, by name and nature, for it weighed a couple of pounds, was nicely formed, of fair colour, and quite as active as some of the bigger creatures brought into the ring, which they certainly did not grace. Another diminutive Yorkie is Mrs Vaughan Fowler's Longbridge Bat, who weighs 2¾ lbs *(1.2kg)* and is particularly smart and lively.'

Champion Ted

From a copy of *Canine World*, published 15 August 1890 in England, comes the following report on Champion Ted. First shown in July 1887, he had won 96 first prizes up to the time of this article's publication:

Our Coloured Portrait

Mrs Foster's Yorkshire Terrier Champion, Ted

'There is not, we venture to asset, a more illustrious canine personage

Above: *A photographic portrait of Mrs M A Foster who owned and campaigned many famous Yorkies under her prefix of Bradford.*

Left: *Mrs Foster's Champion Ted, illustrated in* The Canine World, *1890, and Huddersfield Ben are ancestors of most Yorkies today.*

at present before the public than Mrs Foster's liliputian Yorkshire Terrier luminary, Champion Ted, which adorns our front page this week, and which portrait, in its artistic merit, we hope, is worthy of the illustrious, if diminutive subject it is intended to portray.

'Champion Ted, if not the best specimen that ever lived — a question of a very controversial nature, and one impossible to prove — is at least, no one will deny, the best of his variety living, around whom hangs a halo of fame which falls to the lot of few canine celebrities, let him be of whatever breed he may.

'Some estimate may be formed of the brilliancy of the bench career of this broadacre beauty when we state that Champion Ted has won, against allcomers, no less than 75 first prizes, 15 challenge prizes and 25 cups, specials and other trophies. In his memorable contest for supremacy at Leeds Show the other week, in competing for the non-sporting special, Champion Ted was within a hair's breadth of dethroning his more Goliath rival and hitherto unbeaten king of the canine race, Champion Sir Bedivere, and earned for himself in that feat alone a felicitous distinction of which any ordinary subject of the dog realm might feel justly proud.

'As it was, Ted lowered the colour of such cracks as the Bulldog Champion British Monarch, as well as all the other non-sporting winners at this important Show, polling for this trophy three votes, as against Sir Bedivere's four, and at the hands of a syndicate of seven of the judges, who gave their decision separately and by ballot, which was, therefore, thoroughly unbiased, and a true test of the relative merit of — we may rightly assume — the two best dogs in the world!

'Champion Ted was born on July 20th 1885, and is consequently now five years old and in his prime, and Mrs Foster remarks as "nimble and active now as at any part of his life".

'He came into his present owner's possession in March 1887, when he was about 20 months old, at a time when these lovely drawing-room favourites begin to develop the enormous long silky coat and beautiful tan colouring, of which virtues Champion Ted is the very essence and embodiment. Not only this, but regardless of weight, and especially considering Ted's normal and Herculean figure of 4lbs weight *(1.8kg)* when in "fighting form", he is considered by experts to be the best-headed and most perfect-shaped little gentleman Terrier that ever lived, and therefore not, as some are, a mere handful of hair, which property, to the

17

sacrifice of all others, is sometimes the sole guiding consideration of some in the propagation of these extraordinary little creatures.

'And when we come to Ted's coat, as we have stated, we stand in amazement at its profuseness, . enormous whisker, its rich tan and silky, soft texture, as the little dot of a dog majestically sweeps the ground, as with bridal train, before our gaze.

'Ted was, at the time stated, first espied by two such astute experts in Yorkshire Terrier lore as Mrs Foster's husband and their friend, Mr Birkby, who, at that time, both predicted a glorious future for the dog, and time has proved their judgment to have been strictly correct, and their prophesy amply fulfilled. And although Mrs Foster hesitated at the time to pay the high demand the working-man breeder required for this handful of dogflesh — probably the highest price ever given for a Yorkshire Terrier that had never seen the light or been subjected to the fierce test of show-ring competition — yet, she has never regretted the purchase, and only recently refused the enormous offer, we believe, of 200 guineas for her favourite, which amount was probably several times that she originally paid for the dog.

'As a stud dog, Champion Ted's services have not unnaturally been in great request, at which the dog has also proved himself "facile princeps", and a great success, as already many promising recruits in the regiment of Yorkshire Terriers claim him as their sire.

'In disposition, Champion Ted is most buoyant and merry, and of very cheerful temperament, possessing too, remarkable intelligence and sagacity. Indeed, it seems almost incredible that so many virtues can be crowded into the frame and figure of such a mite. To his mistress he is most devoted, and is seldom out of her presence, and the air of assurance he assumes in protecting her is quite amusing, and if not so imposing, outstrips that of a dutiful Mastiff, and altogether presents a picture

perfectly pantomimic in the utter precocity of this mite-y doggy.

We could relate many interesting incidents of Champion Ted's daily domestic doings, but suffice it to say that his mistress is equally attached to the little mite himself who forms part of her personnel, who shares her breakfast table, her bed, and her bounty everywhere.

In such a notice, of such a noted one — and when ladies are coming to the front in every walk of life, and, in fact, in point of pre-eminence, threaten even the lords of creation with rivalry — it is especially befitting we should say a few words about the owner, a lady than whom there is not a more familiar figure or more respected attendant at our dog shows in any part of the country, from John O'Groats to Lands End, and even to many of our Continental Shows she is equally well known and as much

Bradford, Queen of the Toys (left) in 1896, was the smallest adult show-winning Yorkie ever seen. Ch Ted, when featured in Our Dogs, 1985 (right), had already won 75 firsts and 15 CCs.

respected. Not this only, but Mrs Foster is one of the oldest exhibitors living, and although still only in the prime and robustness of life, she has attended shows and been connected with show dogs to our knowledge for the long period of a quarter of a century, but has, we believe, been a breeder and fancier of several varieties of pet dogs an even longer period, about which, however, we hope to say something at a future period, and, therefore, will reserve any further reference here, except to wish Mrs Foster long life and leisure to enjoy the fruits of a pure, well-spent, and illustrious life, to which she is justly entitled.'

A vital fashion 'accessory'
A further article, published in 'Dogs', 22 January 1895 in England, entitled 'Mrs Langtry and her Yorkshire Terrier', is of interest in tracing the breed's historical role.

The article commences with the statement that few people would know how much Lily Langtry contributed to the breed's popularity. Every lady of that time who thought anything of fashion had a Yorkshire Terrier to accompany her whether walking or driving; in fact no outfit was considered complete without a Yorkshire Terrier in evidence.

The breed's popularity was apparently due to the Jersey Lily's insistence during rehearsals of 'Enemies', a play in which she played the leading role, that a little dog trained to jump and bark at the villain of the piece would go down well with the audience. On the opening night of the play the little Yorkie behaved to perfection. The journalist finishes his article with the following paragraph:

'Before the week was out every

Terrier of this breed — or, indeed, anything approaching or having a probable relative in the Yorkshire Terrier family — was snapped up by eager purchasers. St Martin's Lane, the Seven Dials and Leadenhall Market *(in London)* were inundated with orders, as so many had caught the Yorkshire Terrier fever; indeed, even American cousins were paying dealers' expenses to and fro to Yorkshire to secure them.'

The Yorkshire Terrier Club, UK
This was founded in 1898. Lady Edith Windham Dawson became the Club's Honorary Secretary for several years, and was a great supporter of the breed before World War II. Between 1939 and 1945, the Club's cups and records were deposited in a bank for safe-keeping. After the cessation of hostilities, the late Mrs Ethel Munday, whose Yadnum prefix is

of world renown, on becoming the Club's Secretary, recovered the cups and records. Mrs Munday remained Secretary until her resignation in 1959. During her time, she saw the Club through several difficult times and watched the breed's popularity climb from 931 registrations in the UK in 1948 to 3,244 in 1959.

Popularity
The breed's popularity continued to rise reaching 15,147 registrations in the UK in 1974, with a brief drop in 1977. At the end of 1986, the Yorkshire Terrier with 10,637 registrations is the second most popular breed in the UK.

It is interesting to note that at the first Crufts Dog Show held by the Kennel Club at Olympia in 1948, the Dog CC Champion Weedon of Atherleigh, born 13 September 1945, bred and owned by Mr W Hayes, and the Bitch CC Champion Hebsonisn Jealousy, born 19 March 1946, owned and bred by Mrs M Hebson, were great-great-grandchildren of one of the pre-war top winning Yorkshire

Below: *A notable Yorkshire Terrier in the breed's development, Lady Edith Windham's Champion Brian Boru of Soham, born in 1934.*

Terriers, Ch Invincible of Invincia, owned and bred by Mrs Annie Swan. In the same Kennel Club Stud Book of Shows held so soon after World War II, in addition to Mrs Annie Swan, Lady Edith Windham Dawson exhibited two Yorkies in Belfast, and Mrs Crookshank showed Int Ch Mr Pimm of Johnstounburn just out of the Puppy class, winning two 2nd prizes at the Scottish Kennel Club and Caledonian Shows held in Edinburgh.

The Johnstounburn Legend — the Yorkie in Scotland

Today, Johnstounburn House, a large mansion situated on the outskirts of Edinburgh and now a first class restaurant with a high reputation for quality, was the home for many years of the famous Johnstounburn Yorkshire Terriers whose world-wide reputation was also of the highest quality. It was in Johnstounburn House that the late Mrs M Crookshank bred most of her beautiful Yorkshire Terriers.

All Yorkshire Terrier breeders in Scotland are indebted to Mrs Crookshank for her unselfish devotion to the breeding and exhibiting of our beautiful breed. I have examined many Scottish bred Yorkshire Terrier pedigrees and one common factor which is obvious in them all is the influence of the Johnstounburn breeding. Time and time again this famous affix appears, and in my opinion the most prolific Johnstounburn sire must be Champion Mr Pimm of Johnstounburn.

I am sure that every Yorkshire Terrier person in Scotland involved in breeding must either have owned or used a progeny of this little dog, as his name was carried down through the breed by many Yorkies who became champions in their own right. I will attempt to name a few: Champion Wee Eve of Yadnum, Champion Myrtle of Johnstounburn, Champion Pipit of Johnstounburn, Champion Buranthea's Angel Bright, Champion Prim of Johnstounburn and Champion Buranthea's

Doutelle, also the sire of Champion Pimbron of Johnstounburn.

The Jounstounburn name was now to be carried to further success by this Champion. Pimbron then sired Champion Minerva of Johnstounburn, Champion Lilyhill Pimbronette and Champion My Precious Joss who is the GG Sire of my own little bitch, Champion Craigsbank Blue Cinders. In fact Champion Pimbron of Johnstounburn appears three times as GGG Sire in my own Champion Craigsbank Blue Cinders pedigree, which only underlines the strength of this Johnstounburn line.

Whilst I have so far only mentioned Johnstounburn champions, you can be assured there are many excellent dogs who did not gain a champion title but played a very important part in the Johnstounburn story. In fact, from what I can find from my records, no less than seven Johnstounburn brood bitches produced between them ten champions.

There must be hundreds of people who have enjoyed the prestige of the Johnstounburn name, either in the show ring or just in the pleasure of owning a 'Wee Johnstounburn Yorkie'.

THE USA

The first Yorkie to be bred and recorded in America was in the early 1870's, a dog called Jack bred by J Marriot and sired by Havelock Ex Jessie. I can find no trace of either parent but one can probably assume they came from British stock. Jack was exhibited at a show held in New York in 1878, shown in the over 5lbs (2.3kg) class. During the same year at the Westminster Kennel Club Show, 33 Yorkshire Terriers were exhibited in two classes over and under 5lbs.

Conqueror

Rawson Lee's book, *Terriers*, published 1894, notes that a Yorkshire Terrier, Mrs Troughear's Conqueror, was sold for £250 to a Mrs Emmott of the USA in the 1890's. I find this difficult to

believe, since Conqueror was exhibited in the UK during 1883 when he must have been at least 18 months of age, as he sired a bitch puppy born on 17 July 1882, bred by Mrs Foster and named Floss III.

At the Birmingham Show held on 5/7/8 May 1883, Conqueror won 2nd prize, not however entered in the Yorkshire Terrier class, but in a class held for Toys under 7lbs (3.2kg). At this show, he was offered for sale at £1,000. In June the same year at Gloucester Dog Show, entered under Toy Terriers, Conqueror was on sale at £100, but later in the year at the Horley Dog Show held on 23 and 24 October, Conqueror, entered under the class for Toy Dogs and Bitches not exceeding 8lb (3.6kg) was once again on offer for £1,000. If this is the same dog — and I can find no reason to think otherwise — I feel sure he must have gone to the USA about 1884-5.

Neglected breed

In Mr Shield's *The American Book of the Dog*, published in 1890, there is an article written by Mr P Coombs, a breeder and judge who

Above: *This 19th century engraving is thought to be of the famous Huddersfield Ben, a distant ancestor of Yorkies in the USA.*

was considered an authority on the breed, from which I quote:

'Unfortunately, almost anything in the shape of a Terrier having a long coat, with some shade or effect of blue on the body, fawn or silver (more frequently the latter) colored head and legs, with tail docked and ears trimmed (cropped), was received and admired as a Yorkshire Terrier by most everyone except the few competent judges; and the breed, fashionable as it is, is still much neglected in this country for the reason that its care is not so well understood as that of many other breeds.'

Common origins

In researching the American Yorkshire Terriers, it is interesting to discover that Ch Bradford Harry, the first American Kennel Club Champion on record, was imported from England by Mr Coombs, sired by Crawshaws Bruce, dam Beals Lady; he was purchased from Mrs Foster, and hence carried her prefix of 'Bradford'. Another early import of note was American Champion Halifax Beacon, imported by T W Murphy in 1906.

The pedigrees of these two early American champions prove that, as in the UK, American Yorkies can be traced back to both Huddersfield Ben and Eng Ch Ted.

Early fanciers

Another respected fancier in America in those early days, Mrs Senn, sold several Yorkshire Terriers to Mrs Raymond Mallock. This lady appears to have lived in the USA for many years, but by 1906 her name and address, in Eire, appears in the English Kennel Club Stud Books. Before leaving America, she apparently purchased from Mrs Senn several Yorkies:

Lady Ashton, Ashton Wonder, Ashton Pearl and Ashton Marvel. Ashton Marvel, sired by Halifax Marvel out of an unregistered bitch Nell, has an English Stud Book number (1596E) for 1901. Ashton Marvel's entry in the Stud Book gives his date of birth as June 1898, bred by Mr Briggs, owners Walton and Beard.

Mrs Raymond Mallock showed Yorkies under her prefix of Ashton-More for several years. The last Yorkie exhibited by her, Ashton-More Wee, born 1906, a grandson of Ashton Marvel, was last shown in Cork in 1908.

Popularity

The popularity of the breed has continued to rise steadily for many years, due no doubt to the improvement of the breed achieved by the many dedicated fanciers in the USA.

In 1976 the numbers registered had risen to 20,392. By 1986, the Yorkshire Terrier was the 12th most popular breed in the USA with registrations reaching a total of 32,485.

Below: *This cigarette card, issued in 1914 by Wills, illustrates a good example of the Yorkshire Terrier breed in 1913.*

Chapter Two

CHOOSING AND CARE

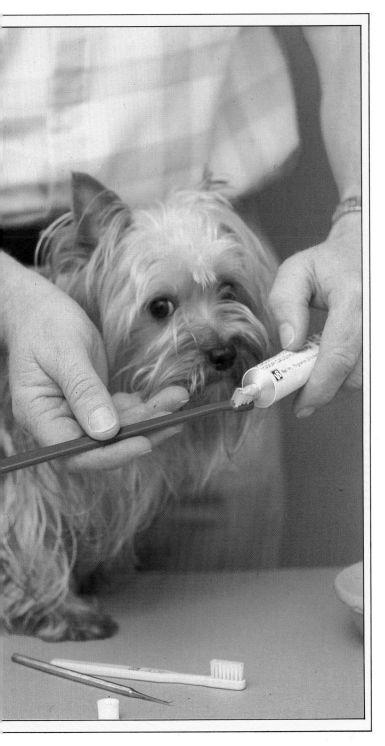

CHARACTERISTICS

The Yorkshire Terrier is, without doubt, one of the most appealing of all Toy Breeds. With its charm and intelligence, the Yorkie is, in spite of its size, full of courage, loyalty and affection. It has an attractive coat, which does not shed, and is always a joy to own.

The Yorkshire Terrier, being a small dog, can be carried easily. Therefore, it is an ideal dog for anyone with a small home and garden or for the flat dweller who enjoys the occasional walk in the park on good days.

CHOOSING A PUPPY

It must never be forgotten that a dog is a living creature. A Yorkshire Terrier will require as much time and care as a small child, especially in view of its small size.

When buying a puppy, make sure you buy from a breeder of repute known for breeding healthy and sound stock. Such breeders can be found by applying to one of the Yorkshire Terrier clubs or your national kennel club (addresses are listed at the back of the book).

The pet Yorkie

If the Yorkshire Terrier is required purely as a pet, a reputable breeder will be prepared to let it go to a new home between 8 and 10 weeks of age. A pet quality puppy will be far cheaper than one of show quality (see Chapter Six for advice on choosing a potential show puppy), which most breeders would not sell until much older. This is because it is quite impossible to guarantee show quality before 6 months of age, especially since the Yorkie at 8 weeks bears little resemblance to the adult dog. The Yorkie puppy is born black. Slight

tan markings are discernible around the face and legs, and the soft, fluffy black coat will show no signs of the silky steel blue to come.

Do not think however that the pet quality puppy is a poor specimen. It will be just as healthy, attractive and intelligent as its litter mates, one of which may be of potential show quality. A reputable breeder will always endeavour to sell as pets stock which may have slight faults, making them unsuitable for breeding from specifically, or for showing. These faults can be very slight indeed; the dog's final size or colour will not affect its value as an attractive pet, which it will surely become. Also, if your Yorkie is kept as a pet, the length of coat is unimportant. Therefore, it is just as easy to bath and groom as any other silky-haired breed. Obviously, the Yorkies' small size is, again, an additional advantage in the task of grooming.

Sex

It is a matter of personal preference which sex you choose. In my opinion, both dog and bitch are equal in intelligence and companionship. Dogs may take a little longer to house train; a bitch will require extra care while in season, which is usually every 6 months.

Selecting an individual

When choosing a puppy from a litter, do not be tempted by the shy retiring individual huddled in the corner. Choose the medium-sized, bouncing extrovert who comes to investigate what is happening. You will then need to make a closer examination. Check the puppy's ears, which should be pink and clean without any odour. A brown discharge could be a sign of ear mites. Its teeth should be clean and white, its eyes bright and alert, and the coat should look and feel clean

Left: *Yorkie puppies are born black with slight tan markings. This litter of two weeks shows the tan markings clearly.*

Below: *A charming pet with pleasing coat and colour. The topknot and face furnishings are cut short for convenience.*

and healthy. Check that nails are short.

Do not hesitate to ask the breeder any questions, no matter how insignificant. Most breeders will welcome your interest.

Documents

Having chosen your puppy, ask the breeder for a diet sheet, and make a note of the type of food and the times the puppy is usually fed. If you keep to the same food and feeding times for the first few days, the chances of an upset stomach will be reduced. Also, make a note of the dates when the puppy was treated for worms.

A receipt with the puppy's pedigree and, if required, the kennel club registration paper should be available at the time of purchase, although it is often the practice of breeders to withold registration of pet stock and to endorse the pedigree 'not to be bred'. This is an attempt to prevent unsuitable stock being used for breeding, thereby ensuring a constant improvement in the breed.

The registration papers will consist of either an application form to register the dog, which you should complete and send to your kennel club with the appropriate fee, or a Registration Certificate

Above: *The puppy is safe and happy in a warm corner away from draughts, enclosed in a wire pen with paper on the floor.*

where the dog has already been named by the breeder but ownership needs to be transferred to you.

BRINGING THE PUPPY HOME

Equipment

Certain preparations are necessary before you bring your puppy home. A small strong cardboard box cut down in the front, without any dangerous staples, makes an excellent bed. Young puppies will chew anything so the cardboard box can be renewed as necessary. When the puppy has passed its chewing stage, a permanent basket or bed can then be purchased from any good pet shop.

The box should be placed in a safe, warm, draught-proof corner out of the family's way. Fill the box with a warm, woolly blanket, vet bed or soft cushion. Young puppies require plenty of sleep and rest without disturbance, even during the day, so do make sure its bed is in a quiet corner away from family disturbances.

It is advisable to surround the bed with a fine wire mesh, similar to a child's play pen. These puppy pens are available at most pet stores or can easily be made at home. But make sure the wire mesh is fine enough to prevent the Yorkie puppy getting its head caught between the wire. The pen should be high enough to prevent the puppy climbing out, and also be big enough to enable plenty of newspaper to be left outside its bed where it will relieve itself on waking. Puppies rarely, if ever, soil their beds.

You will need a feeding bowl with a solid base, and a water bowl always full of fresh water, left in a safe place.

Very young puppies do not require much combing and brushing, but it is a good idea to get them used to being combed and brushed at an early age. You will need a soft, pure bristle brush and a steel comb with fairly wide teeth. Nylon brushes or pin brushes are quite unsuitable for the Yorkie's silky coat, as these will break the hair.

Although puppies must not be allowed on the street on a lead until fully inoculated (see Chapter Three on Vaccination), a soft collar and lead is useful for training the puppy in the garden. Later, for road walks, a strong collar and lead are necessary. Dogs should always be exercised on a lead in built-up areas.

In choosing toys, always make sure they are too big for the puppy's mouth. Small toys can

Right: *Use a soft, pure bristle brush and a steel comb, as illustrated here, to start gently grooming the young puppy.*

Below: *An easily renewable bed for the early days with blanket, hot-water bottle and ticking clock, which must be closed.*

become lodged in the mouth or throat causing great discomfort. A tightly knotted pair of nylon tights or stockings always make an acceptable plaything.

SETTLING IN

The success of the new arrival in the family depends completely on the owner's preparation and early training. Puppies, like young children, must be taught from a very early age just what is expected of them. On the puppy's first arrival at its new home, everything will be strange and slightly frightening. Until now, the puppy will have had the companionship of its litter brothers and sisters so will be quite unused to being alone. But it will quickly adapt to the warmth and companionship of its new home and owner.

The first night

So, a young puppy's first night in your home will be its first experience of being alone without the warmth and comfort of its litter brothers and sisters. Needless to say, it is not going to enjoy it. Feeling cold and lonely, the puppy will undoubtedly start howling, and of course the longer it howls the more lonely and cold it will become. Should you scold and leave alone in the hope that the puppy will tire itself out? Or should you pick it up, soothe and take it to your own bed?

Both these solutions are really quite unsatisfactory. On no account go into the room to scold the puppy. This will not worry it at all, as all it really wants is your company. Stand outside the door and scold the puppy in a firm voice. If you give in you will have nights of trouble, and unless you are prepared for it to sleep in your bedroom for all time, do not allow it to do so 'just this once'. Think about the long term situation.

By far the best idea in minimizing the 'first night' problem is to provide a comfortable bed with substitutes for the litter mates the puppy will be missing. An old-

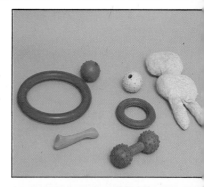

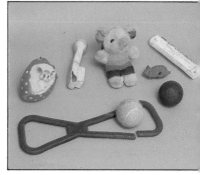

Top: *These are all safe toys of the right size for a Yorkie puppy. None of these can be splintered and the soft toy is free from any dangerous appendages.*

Above: *Tennis balls can fray when chewed; plastic toys can splinter; the soft toy's eyes can be swallowed and large balls can lodge in the mouth.*

fashioned hot water bottle (not rubber as the puppy may chew it), securely wrapped in a blanket, should be placed in the puppy's box. This will provide additional warmth. A softly ticking, **closed** travelling alarm clock will provide a substitute for the heartbeats of the missing litter. A child's soft toy will also help to console the puppy on the loss of its cosy and warm litter mates.

After two or three nights, the puppy will learn that it is bedtime and will quickly accept its bed and pen as its own domain.

Vitamin Sources

Vit A: — Found in egg, milk, butter, animal fats and cod liver oil — necessary for resistance to disease and for growth.

Vit B: — Wholemeal bread, eggs, vegetables and yeast — this vitamin is required regularly to tone the nervous system and give energy.

Vit C: — Fresh fruit — i.e. orange juice and vegetables which purify the blood.

Vit D: — Liver and cod liver oil — for good bones.

Vit E: — Oats, wheatgerm, olive oil and lettuce — for fertility.

SAFETY

Never forget that young puppies are used to being on the level and will fall if left on a chair or table. Young children should only be allowed to hold the puppy while they are sitting on the floor. Take care when opening or shutting doors; puppies move very quickly and it is easy to catch their feet. All electrical plugs and wires must be kept out of the puppy's reach.

FEEDING

All puppies and growing dogs need more food a day than the fully grown dog. Four meals a day are necessary when young. When fully mature, one, or at the most two meals a day are sufficient. The quantities will depend also on the amount of energy it expends in exercise. For the puppy, the correct amount should be given to you by the breeder who will know from experience how many times a day

and how much is required for maximum growth and care.

The types of food needed to promote a healthy and sound body are as follows:-

Protein is essential. This is obtained in all dairy foods, meat, fish, poultry and rabbit, all of which will promote a good body.

Fat, starch and sugar are needed to provide energy, calcium and phosphorous, also contained in dairy foods.

Liver, parsley, seaweed powder, kidney and wholemeal bread will provide iron.

Vitamins are important to dogs as well as to ourselves. The chart gives the source of these vitamins in natural foods. Most of these vitamins can, of course, be obtained in powder or tablet form. I personally prefer natural sources.

Puppy diets

As mentioned before, it is important, on purchasing your puppy, to obtain a diet sheet from the breeder. Yorkies vary on their daily dietary needs, and the breeder will know exactly how much your puppy requires to ensure a healthy and happy adulthood.

Feed at the same time every day. do not at any time give cooked bones; these will splinter. All bones should be removed from rabbit, fish and chicken for the same reason. A small raw beef bone is safe, greatly appreciated and will prevent the puppy chewing other things about the house. A vitamin supplement may be added to the feed once a day. All food should be served at a reasonable temperature, never too hot nor frozen, and served in a quiet atmosphere. Too much noise can prevent a puppy from eating. Do not leave food down. If not eaten within 10 minutes, remove until the next meal. Dogs do not chew, so it is quite natural for them to bolt their food very quickly. Dogs and puppies should always rest after a meal.

The adult Yorkie
In recommending the quantity of food to be fed daily to your adult Yorkie, several facts must be considered. If your Yorkie is a pet given limited exercise, it will not require as much food as the country dog who is free-running all day. A busy stud dog requires extra food, as does a brood bitch, but as a rough guide the usual requirements are considered to be ½oz (14.2g) of food for 1lb (453.6g) of body weight plus biscuit or cereal a day. To give exact amounts is quite useless; like people, some dogs eat a lot and keep thin, whilst others with very little food get fat. It is up to each owner to gauge the amount suitable for his or her own Yorkshire Terrier.

Types of ready-made food
With the great advance in the quality of canned dog food, for convenience and to save time, the well-established makers of dog food and puppy meal can be relied on to provide nutritious and substantial meals. Quantities are given according to the dog's size and/or age.

Meal or dried dog foods are also available. Once again, the well-established brands are considered

---
Diet for a puppy

From 2-4 months. Give meals at regular times according to the daily routine of the household.

Breakfast: Any cereal with warm milk (not *Allbran*) with a little honey or Glucose added
OR
Scrambled egg with a little well toasted wholemeal bread
OR
Egg with grated cheese and wholemeal bread

Midday: Any of the following:
Raw beef, Cooked beef, lamb, rabbit, all cut up into small pieces; cooked chicken (no bones); white fish (no bones) plus a little biscuit or wholemeal bread or grated carrot.

Late Afternoon: Warm milk with a digestive biscuit or toasted wholemeal bread

Supper: Same as Midday

Vitamin/mineral supplement given daily

Before bed, the same as late afternoon snack, but not too much milk otherwise you will undoubtedly find a puddle in the morning.

Fresh clean water must **always** be available.

to be nutritious and satisfying for health and growth. Some are fed dry whilst others require to be served moist.

As the Yorkie requires such a small amount of food a day, I personally consider that its food should be of the very best quality.

TRAINING

House training/breaking

One of the most important things to understand and always remember is that young puppies have very little control, but if raised under good and clean conditions most have a natural instinct to be clean. Very rarely, even from three weeks of age, will a puppy soil its bed if it is possible to find another spot.

A puppy will soon decide where it wishes to relieve itself. It is therefore up to you to make sure it chooses the right spot. The 'right spot' to start with can be newspaper put down in the same place, in any room where the puppy is running free. You will soon learn by the puppy's behaviour the signs of wanting to relieve itself, which are always the same. It will firstly sniff the floor circling round to find the right spot. When you see it doing this, pick the puppy up and take it outside. Stay with the puppy until it has done what is expected, then praise lavishly. If you leave the puppy, it will just follow you. A few minutes spent with it will achieve far more. Puppies should be taken outside immediately after they wake and after every meal before resting. However, puppies should not be taken outside in wet weather; in this case put it on some pieces of newspaper, making sure it stays there until relieved. Again, remember to praise the puppy.

If from an early age the puppy is trained to use newspaper, this training will be of great use to owners living in flats when it is not always possible, due to bad weather, to go for those early and late walks. If you always place the newspaper in the same place, the puppy will soon understand its use.

The occasional mistakes will occur; paper, grass and carpet will all seem very similar to the puppy. To remove the possibility of stains on the carpet, pour or spray fizzy soda water onto the spot, leave for a few seconds and then soak up with tissue or a paper kitchen towel.

In addition to training a dog to be clean at home, it is equally important that it is trained to behave properly in public places. It is unlawful for a dog to foul pavements or public footpaths, so it must be taught to use the gutter, grass or rough ground. Always carry a plastic bag or 'poop-scoop' to remove any accidents immediately; you can be fined for failure to do so.

Puppy training

The owner's early behaviour and understanding of a puppy will establish its health and character as

Below: *These two 'poop-scoops' are equally effective and hygienic. The small one is obviously more portable.*

an adult dog. For the first few days, while the puppy is assimilating so many new experiences, it will spend most of its time exploring the new surroundings, eating and sleeping. Nevertheless, it will need to learn several things quite quickly, bearing in mind that the puppy will have very little idea, if any, of what is expected of it.

Firstly, teach the puppy its name. Call it, and when it comes to you, reward it with praise and a titbit. Within a very short time it will recognize its name immediately and you will have established the first link towards obedience.

On no account must you call its name for any unpleasant reason; it is vital for its protection and your peace of mind that when it is called by name and comes to you, the word is only associated with pleasurable experiences.

The word 'No' must be used in a firm voice whenever the puppy does wrong. Make your tone of voice very stern. Dogs understand the **tone** of the human voice, not the word. So in praising or blaming, your voice must be quite distinctive in tone.

Above: *Begin lead training by allowing the puppy to wander around wearing the collar with the lead trailing.*

Below: *In this way, the Yorkie puppy will soon become accustomed to the collar and lead. Always watch where the puppy goes.*

Lead training

Once the puppy has learnt its name and is clean and regular in its habits, the training to walk on a collar and lead is the next essential. To achieve this, use the soft collar and lead purchased for use in the garden. Let the puppy get used to the collar first by making it wear it during the day while it runs loose around the garden. When the collar no longer bothers the puppy, attach the lead and once again let it wander on its own but always where you can watch it, otherwise the lead could get caught by various obstacles thereby causing distress or even injury. After a few minutes running free, pick up the end of the lead and go where the puppy chooses. As soon as it realizes that it is no longer free, the puppy will buck and struggle. At this point, stand quite still and eventually it will stop struggling. When it does, very gently pull the lead towards you calling the puppy's name. When it comes, which it will eventually, reward the puppy with much praise and a titbit. Only when it ceases to struggle and will come to you

Above: *After running free, pick up the end of the lead and go where the puppy chooses. Then pull the lead towards you.*

Below: *After a few days of patient training, the puppy will be happy to trot along on the lead, as illustrated.*

quickly when pulled is the time to walk slowly away from it giving the lead a gentle tug and calling its name. If the puppy sits down, just wait. Do not pull but wait until it stands and try again. Five minutes a day is ample; lessons of short duration given often are by far the most satisfactory.

Lastly, in all training, do be patient, affectionate and understanding. Give the dog plenty of time and it will learn and understand all that is required of it. Also, do spend some time just playing with it for fun; a few games will be enjoyed by both you and the puppy.

Above: *A puppy moving well on a soft nylon collar and lead. Walk the puppy on your left side if you intend to show it.*

Below: *It is vital to be patient in lead training; it is a gradual process of learning with just a few minutes spent daily.*

──Combination collar and lead──

Right and below: *A recommended light combination collar and lead with a slip ring for adjusting collar size, a locking ring to prevent choking and escape, plus a swivel which prevents tangling.*

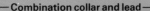

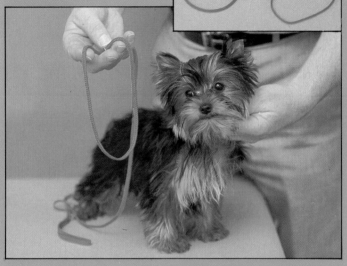

Below: *The collar can be made any size using the slip ring. There are no buckles for the puppy's hair to get caught up in.*

Below: *Adjust the collar so that it is comfortable but tight enough to prevent escape. Then slide the locking ring down.*

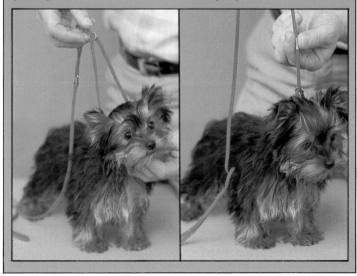

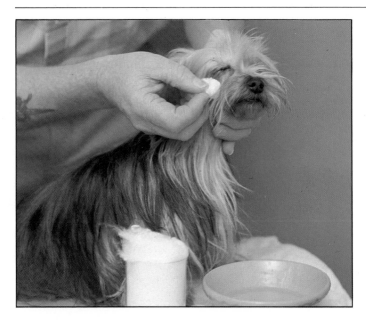

HOME HEALTH CARE

You will need to establish a daily care routine of the puppy's eyes, ears, teeth, feet and coat. It is advisable to continue this routine throughout your Yorkie's adult life to ensure maximum health. It will also enable you to detect any problems at an early stage that may require veterinary attention.

Eyes
The eyes should be bathed using cotton wool dipped in cool water or a mild solution of Boracic dissolved in cool water, to clear any mucus from the corners. An abundance of facial hair can cause problems — see veterinary care, page 54.

Ears
These should be examined to make sure they are clean and sweet smelling. Any discharge or odour will require veterinary attention.

Excess hair in the ears can be a problem in the Yorkshire Terrier, especially in puppyhood. Pluck a few hairs at a time between finger and thumb when grooming (see Chapter Three on Common Ailments and Diseases).

Above: *Check your Yorkie's eyes daily. Bathe gently, as shown, to remove any discharge using a clean swab for each eye.*

Teeth
It is important to get your Yorkie puppy accustomed to having its teeth cleaned at a young age, at least once a week. There are many special dog toothbrushes and toothpaste available, and your veterinarian will advise you on what to choose (see Chapter Three on Common Ailments and Diseases). Regular brushing, combined with regular scaling and polishing by the veterinarian throughout its life, plus a regular supply of raw beef bones, will help to preserve the Yorkshire Terrier's teeth.

Retention of baby teeth can cause long-term problems for the Yorkie (see Chapter Three, Common Ailments and Diseases). The permanent teeth are fully errupted between six and nine months of age. Check to see if there are any baby teeth left at this stage. A full complement of permanent teeth amounts to 42. In the upper jaw there should be six incisors and two canines, one on

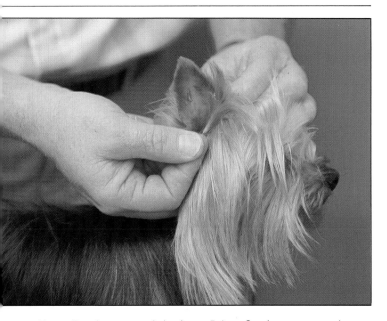

Above: *Examine ears regularly; they should be pink and clean. Carefully pluck out excess hair a little at a time, as shown.*

Below: *Starting at a very early age, clean the Yorkie's teeth weekly using a soft toothbrush and canine toothpaste.*

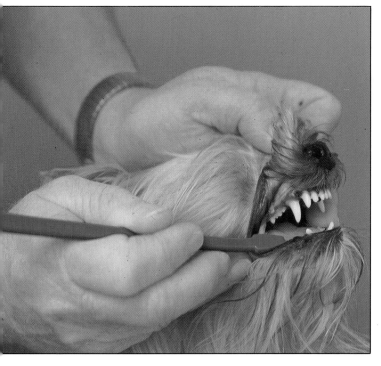

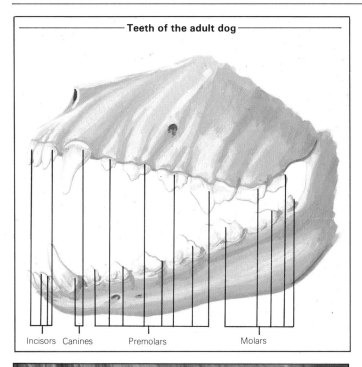

Teeth of the adult dog

Incisors Canines Premolars Molars

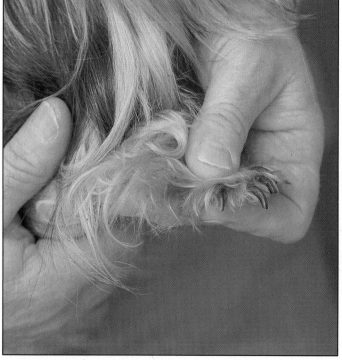

each side of the incisors. Behind each canine are four premolars and two molars on each side, making 20 teeth in all. In the lower jaw, the distribution is identical except for the molars, of which there are three on each side, making 22 teeth.

Consult your veterinarian if you discover any abnormality.

Feet
Check the pads for any foreign

Left: *The canine mouth has 42 teeth: upper jaw 6 incisors 2 canines 8 premolars 4 molars; the lower, same but 2 extra molars.*

Below left: *In order to trim these long nails, firmly press the pads between your thumb and fore-finger to extend the nails.*

Below: *This guillotine nail cutter is far easier to use than ordinary clippers. Trim carefully to avoid cutting the quick.*

bodies or cuts. Nails should be clipped short otherwise they will grow too long and could easily be torn off.

Inside the nail is a fleshy part called the 'quick' which, if cut, will bleed and cause your dog pain. Use the guillotine type of nail clippers and carefully trim the nail a little at a time. It should be possible to see the quick if the nail is not too dark in colour. If you do cause the nail to bleed, a dab of permanganate of potash or a styptic pencil will stop the bleeding quite quickly.

If you are at all doubtful about this operation, visit your veterinarian when necessary.

Coat
Brush the coat daily with a soft bristle brush. Make sure you brush right down to the skin, and then comb the coat thoroughly, not forgetting the ear fringes and beard. See Chapter Five for detailed guidance on bathing, drying and preparation of the show coat.

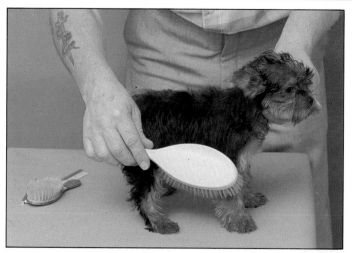

1

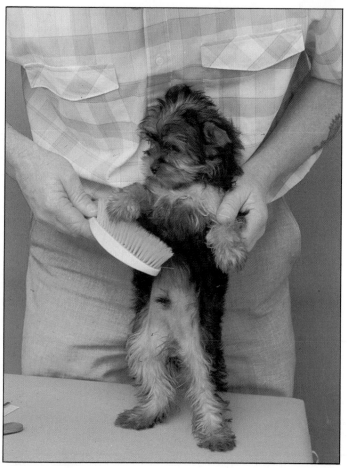

2

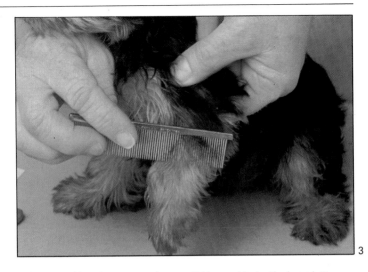

3

1 *Start brushing the puppy early — it will soon become accustomed to it and, given a special hug, will even look forward to it.*

2 *The puppy's tummy must not be forgotten, especially with males. Hold the puppy firmly and brush upwards away from vital parts.*

3 *Use a wide-toothed comb to groom the puppy's feet and legs. Hold the hair close to the skin to gently tease out any knots.*

4 *Hold the puppy's head firmly to gently comb face furnishings. It may be necessary to sponge the face first to remove any food.*

4

TRAVELLING

Above: *This travelling box is safe and comfortable and can also be used indoors as a safe and snug bed for the dog.*

One of the worst aspects of travelling with dogs in the car is the fact that so many suffer from travel sickness. I have discovered from experience that if you get puppies used to car travel between seven and nine weeks of age, they very rarely suffer from car sickness when older. I have also found that dogs prone to sickness are less likely to suffer if they are boxed with good ventilation and their vision forward-looking only. The overhead movement of trees, sky, lamp-posts or pylons flashing by seems to disturb them, often causing nervousness and sickness.

It is much safer for small dogs to travel in covered cages or boxes. I often hear pet owners say that they consider it cruel to put dogs in these boxes; how wrong they are. If they are provided with a box or cage made comfortable with a warm blanket in winter, and a cool layer of cotton in the summer, all small dogs will come to regard their box as their own special property. With the door left open at home, they will retire voluntarily to their refuge whenever sleepy or needing a rest.

On a long car journey, safe in its familiar box or cage, the Yorkshire Terrier will be both secure and relaxed. The driver will also be secure in the knowledge that there is no possibility of a sprightly youngster jumping on it or, if it is necessary to brake quickly, that no injury will come to the dog.

These same cages or boxes are also invaluable for transporting Yorkies to dog shows if, as so often happens, the weather is cold, wet or windy. The dogs will keep warm and dry on passage from the car to the show site.

The size of the box or cage is important; it must be large enough for a Yorkie to stand up and turn round. Always make sure the fastenings are secure.

OLD AGE IN THE YORKIE

The old Yorkie will have far less stamina and require only the minimum of exercise. Eyes can fail and hearing become impaired. The skin becomes loose on the body, the pigment on the nose may also fade with age and often the dog will start to put on weight.

There are many ways of keeping the old dog happy. Established routines of feeding and exercise

Above: *An open cage which is also collapsible — very useful for car travel, especially when the weather is hot.*

Below: *Strive to be a loving and responsible owner to your devoted companion throughout its life, especially in its later days.*

should be continued but with a reduction in food as the amount of exercise lessens. Make sure your old Yorkie has a warm and comfortable bed; do not let it get wet and keep it out of draughts.

Old age in dogs is often accompanied by various illnesses, both minor and severe. Nearly all can be treated by modern drugs, but the time will come when you have to decide when its life must end. Many owners prolong the so-called 'life' of their pets for selfish reasons; a point is reached when the owner is prolonging death not life. As a loving and responsible owner, the last kindness you can give your devoted friend of many years is a quick and painless release from possible suffering and a life without any 'living'.

Chapter Three

VETERINARY CARE

The first visit
The healthy puppy
Pet health insurance
Common ailments and diseases

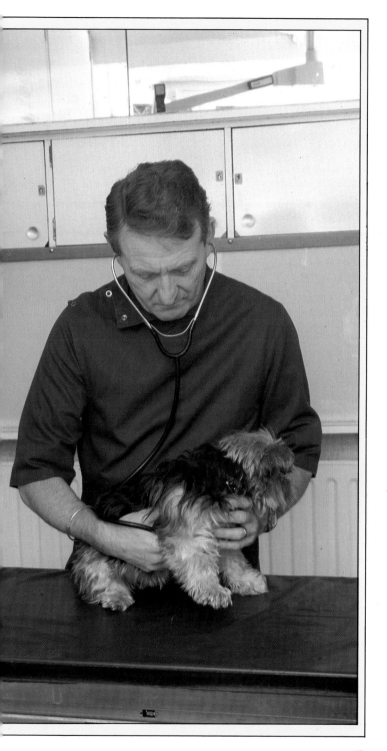

AFTER choosing your puppy, the next major decision is your choice of veterinarian. How do you do it? If you live fairly close to the breeder (or pet store), they will be able to help with the choice of veterinarian, but if the puppy has travelled some distance you will then have to depend on Yellow Pages and the recommendation of other dog owners.

Before collecting your puppy, it is worthwhile taking a walk in the local parks and asking one or two people exercising their dogs. The police are another good source of names of veterinarians. The name that crops up most frequently is probably the one to try first. Telephone the practice or go in before you have even acquired the puppy and find out the procedure. If the impression is favourable, that is the practice to go to. If not, try others in the area until you find one that suits you.

Fees and premises will vary. Do not be influenced too much by either initially; the quality of the service, availability at unsocial hours and willingness to discuss problems are probably of more importance.

THE FIRST VISIT

The main reason for this visit is to check the general health of the puppy and to examine it for any sign of congenital or hereditary deformity. It is often the time for the commencement of vaccination. The veterinary surgeon will probably examine the puppy very thoroughly in order to make sure that you have purchased a healthy one. Do not be upset if the puppy appears to object to part of the examination. It does not understand the reason for it and it will be very strange for it. However, it is essential that the puppy's temperature is taken and its ears, eyes, heart, joints and abdomen are all checked.

What is the veterinarian looking for when he or she carries out this examination? Apart from signs of enteritis and general health, he or she will also be looking to see if there are any specific problems. He will examine the skin since certain types of mange, including ear mange, are not uncommon in Yorkshire Terrier puppies. Examining the skeleton, even in such a young puppy, can sometimes reveal slipping kneecaps which can lead to lameness (see page 54). Also a deformity of the skull, due to lack of closure of the bones on the top of the head, is not uncommon. This is called molera. If you have a male puppy, the veterinarian will check to see that both testicles are descended and in the scrotum.

The discussion

The veterinarian will ask you questions about the puppy's feeding and behaviour pattern. Do not be afraid to discuss any worries you may have at this stage. He or she will check on any worming programme and probably suggest one that may vary from that which the breeder has suggested.

Puppies with problems

What happens if the veterinarian finds a problem which may have been present from birth? Deformity of the knee joint causing slipping of the kneecap is an example of this, but there are others in Yorkshire Terrier puppies. The problem may not only have been present from birth (congenital) but may be hereditary and the veterinarian may suggest that the puppy is returned to the breeder. This is one reason why it is worthwhile ensuring that the puppy receives its first veterinary examination within a short time of your acquiring it. If you do not feel you want to return the puppy, despite the fact that it may have serious abnormalities, do not be afraid to discuss this with the veterinarian. He or she is working in your best interests but will not be unsympathetic. Nonetheless, the veterinarian has a job to do and would not be doing it properly if he or she did not explain to you the problems that might arise as the puppy gets older.

THE HEALTHY PUPPY

Having passed the physical examination, the veterinarian will now discuss feeding and general management, training, worming and vaccination with you. Remember that the veterinarian's fee covers the consultation costs, and consultation means what it says. Any worries, doubts or problems you may have should be discussed at this time, no matter how trivial you may think them. Do not be afraid of making a list of questions you may want to ask. These may include breeding. Do you want to breed from your Yorkie? Here, size plays a part. The current trend within the breed is for ever smaller, and thus more expensive, animals. But remember that these are often the bitches that can have problems when whelping (giving birth). Many novice owners will acquire a male puppy and feel that they would like to show it and breed from it. This is not quite as easy as it first appears and the veterinarian will be willing to advise on various aspects.

Vaccination
If the puppy is old enough and fit enough, vaccination may be commenced on your first visit. Do not worry if the vaccination programme appears at variance with that suggested by the breeder or that of other friends with puppies. Vaccination programmes today are individually tailored to the puppy. Infection in any particular area, the age of the puppy and other factors are taken into account

Below: *It is most important to arrange a visit to a veterinarian as soon as possible after acquiring your Yorkie puppy.*

by the veterinarian.

Most puppies are vaccinated from about eight weeks of age. Modern canine vaccines usually involve at least two injections, with the second one given at around three months. These injections give good protection against the major canine diseases, but remember that a vaccine that gives 100% protection against canine diseases has not yet been invented. The diseases covered by vaccination are several in number. They include Canine Parvo-virus disease, which is transmitted by a very resistant virus that can live away from the body for long periods of time. It causes depression, vomiting and diarrhoea, often with blood. Treatment involves intensive care and intravenous fluid therapy and sometimes is not successful. Vaccination gives good protection but must be boosted annually.

Distemper is another virus disease. Although now less common than in the past, it still occurs in epidemic form from time to time. Vomiting and diarrhoea can be signs but usually the animal appears to have a 'cold' with runny eyes and nose, often with a cough. Later nervous signs can develop with twitching or even fits and paralysis. A form of distemper

Above: *Set up some sort of foolproof system to remind you when annual booster vaccinations are due, for maximum protection.*

causes hardening of all the pads, hence the name 'Hardpad'. A yearly booster is recommended.

Canine Hepatitis is another disease which dogs can be protected against by today's multivalent vaccines. This disease is better described as canine adenovirus[1] infection since it often causes more problems with the kidneys than the liver and is caused by canine adenovirus[1]. Infection is contracted from both faeces and urine and recovered dogs may act as carriers. The virus may also affect the lungs and cause a respiratory form of the disease, but this is more commonly caused by canine adenovirus type [2] which is part of the cough complex of diseases.

Vaccination against the diseases caused by both canine adenovirus[1] and canine adenovirus[2] is achieved by the use of a vaccine made from CAV[2] which is safer in that it does not cause eye complications, which sometimes did occur when CAV[1] vaccines were used.

Leptospirosis is a bacterial rather

than a virus disease. It is incorporated in the canine vaccination programme since serious illness can result from infection, and it can also affect humans. There are two forms in the dog. Leptospira icter-haemorrhagiae causes fever, jaundice and severe depression and can be passed to humans. The other form in the dog, Leptospira canicola, is also called 'lamp-post disease' and affects the kidneys. Although, unlike virus diseases, Leptospiral diseases can be treated with antibiotics, prevention is better than cure. Again an annual booster is recommended.

Infectious rhinotracheitis, the so-called 'cough syndrome', is popularly known as 'kennel cough' although it can affect animals that have never been near kennels. It is a highly infectious condition caused by a mixture of viruses and bacteria. Some multivalent vaccines on the market cover the viral components and there is also an intranasal vaccine which covers the most important bacterial component, Bordatella. This is a useful vaccine to have if there is an outbreak of cough in an area or if you are about to board your dog. Protection only lasts for about six months. In the United States an injectable Bordatella vaccine is available but this is not available in the UK.

Rabies vaccination is not usually carried out in Britain unless the puppy is intended for export. With the strict quarantine laws, the UK is rabies free. But this cannot be said for many countries of the world where puppies receive their rabies shots at or about the same time as their other inoculations. Today rabies vaccination, like all other canine inoculations, involves the animal in no risk at all of contracting the disease.

PET HEALTH INSURANCE

Several excellent pet health insurance schemes are available today, particularly those from the specialist companies. These policies, although not covering routine vaccination, worming, whelping and dental prophylaxis, certainly cover all the unexpected veterinary bills as well as chronic conditions up to the insured limit for any condition. Remember that veterinary expertise is rapidly expanding and conditions that were untreatable a few years ago are now regularly treated. Cancer is but one example of this. This expertise and care has to be paid for and unfortunately veterinary fees are increasing. Talk with your veterinarian about pet health insurance; at present premium levels it is a bargain!

COMMON AILMENTS AND DISEASES

Although the Yorkshire Terrier is the smallest breed within the Terrier group, it is nevertheless a true Terrier and is therefore quite a hardy and trouble-free little dog. However, Yorkies can be afflicted with certain general 'doggie' ailments and a few that, for various reasons, are almost specific to the breed. The latter are highlighted by italics in the following text.

Anal problems
Problems affecting the back door of the bowel are common in many dogs today and Yorkies are no exception. Both dogs and bitches have two small scent glands which lie on either side of the anus and are normally emptied when the dog passes faeces. Sometimes trouble occurs, and the anal glands can fill up and cause problems.

Usually the first sign is that your pet will appear to be licking itself excessively behind or else scooting or dragging its bottom along the ground. *Anal sac problems may be caused by worms, diarrhoea or infection and a visit to the veterinarian is a reasonable precaution. If it is just simple impaction of the glands, he or she may show you how to empty them yourself. Once the trouble has started some Yorkies will develop a fixation about their anal glands and* often bite and chew in the groin or at the base of their tail. In these cases, if persistent, the veterinarian may advise surgical removal of the glands in order to provide a permanent solution to the problem.

Faecal Matts

These are a common anal problem in the Yorkshire Terrier and practically unknown in other breeds. Due to the long hair, bits of faeces will get stuck around the anus and quickly cause soreness to this sensitive area. Adult dogs are less often affected than puppies, when the condition can be acute in onset and the puppy may be very distressed, running around and trying to attack its rear end. If the problem has been present for more than an hour or two, the stool will have hardened and removal can be extremely difficult. Bathing with lots of warm soapy water and much massage will do the trick, but sometimes a visit to the veterinarian can become necessary. It can be prevented by carefully trimming the hair around the anal area.

Bowel problems

The most obvious signs are vomiting and diarrhoea. An upset of the bowel is one of the most common illnesses of dogs and Yorkshire Terriers are no exception. Puppies eat all manner of foreign material and insult the bowel. Other causes can be infections, poisons,

parasites and allergies as well as foreign bodies such as pebbles, bits of plastic toys etc. A radical change of diet or too many titbits can also be a cause. A good first-aid measure is to limit but not prevent fluid intake and to starve the animal for 24 hours. If there then is no improvement, it should be taken to the veterinarian. If the dog vomits or passes blood, the veterinarian should be contacted without delay. A faecal sample is often a good idea to help with diagnosis, particularly in the case of puppies.

Colic

This is another condition often common in the Yorkshire Terrier. Principally, it affects the very young and the very old. Puppies at around weaning will often over-eat and become distressed with wind. One of the medical preparations of babies' gripe water, or alternatively a preparation containing charcoal will often relieve the condition but if the puppy is very distressed, a visit to the veterinarian is necessary. Colic in the elderly Yorkie is often due to the inability of the old bowel to contract in a normal manner, and in consequence after a meal the poor dog 'blows up' with wind. The

Below: *A veterinarian making a routine check on the heart and lungs. Thankfully, heart problems are rare in the Yorkshire Terrier.*

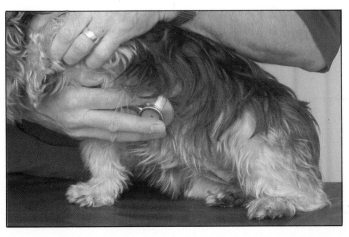

veterinarian can do much to help, so do not be afraid to discuss the problem with him or her.

Haemorrhagic enteritis
Simple enteritis, vomiting and diarrhoea, can in many small breeds of dogs quickly progress to the haemorrhagic form when the poor animal is passing blood from both ends. Canine parvo-virus is often the cause of this in puppies but other causes, including toxaemia, shock and infection, can be responsible in adult dogs. Immediate contact with your veterinarian is essential. The dog usually wants to drink copiously but this will only make the vomiting, and hence the condition, much worse.

Breathing problems
Puppies and adult dogs of many breeds can suffer from infections of the cough complex which result in difficulty in breathing. In addition, Yorkshire Terriers are prone to two conditions which can cause distressed respiration. One is a restricted airway or *elongated soft palate,* often found in very tiny animals, which results in the dog snorting and snuffling since the soft palate overlies the entrance to the

windpipe. Sometimes this can be associated with chronically enlarged tonsils and the veterinarian may advise operation. The second one is a *collapsed trachea.* This is not an uncommon condition in the Yorkshire Terrier and can occur at any age. The little cartilage rings which ensure that the windpipe is kept open collapse due to an inherent defect and result in great difficulty in breathing. This is not easy to treat particularly in the older, obese animal.

Heart problems
Heart problems are not common in the Yorkshire Terrier except in the older, fat Yorkie. Beware — one of the first signs is a chronic cough.

Ear problems
Ear problems are relatively common in Yorkie puppies and the veterinarian will probably spend some time in examining them.

Otodectic mange (ear mites) is relatively common and starts with itchy ears in the puppy and quickly progresses to a lot of brown smelly wax. There are many preparations available from the veterinarian that will soon clear the trouble. Neglected, it can progress to chronic otitis or so-called 'canker'.

Hair growth in the ears is another problem that can be difficult in the Yorkshire Terrier, particularly the puppy. An abundance of hair prevents the natural shaking out of

Below: *The veterinarian will check your Yorkie's ears carefully, since Yorkie puppies are fairly susceptible to ear problems.*

old wax and this invites infection. Pulling out a few hairs at a time when grooming is a good idea.

Eyes

Yorkshire Terriers' eyes are relatively trouble free, but the abundance of hair around the face can lead to irritation and result in chronic conjunctivitis and tear staining. Judicious trimming and the use of a rubber band on the topknot help to prevent the condition. Bath with cold water in the morning and avoid preparations such as cold tea and other home remedies. If you are worried, ask your veterinarian.

Distichiasis is not common in the Yorkie but involves extra eyelashes causing pain and irritation. These have to be surgically removed.

Fits and *Collapse*

A dog in a fit is unconscious and not aware of what is happening. Fits occur for many reasons and are much more traumatic for the owner than the dog. They usually only last for a few seconds but urination and defaecation can occur. When the dog comes out of the fit, it can neither see nor hear properly for a short while and therefore may bite even the owner in self-defence. Fits in puppies can be due to infections (such as distemper), worms, colic and many other causes.

Collapse in the Yorkshire Terrier can sometimes be due to a lack of circulating blood sugar. Therefore any case of fitting or collapse should be reported to the veterinarian.

Lamenesses

Patella luxation (slipping kneecaps, slipping stifle) is a relatively common condition in the Yorkie and often results in the intermittent lifting of one or both hindlegs when walking or running. It is possibly recessively inherited and therefore it is sensible not to breed from afflicted animals. Today, veterinary orthopaedics are such that corrective surgery is usually extremely successful.

Von Perthes' disease (Auscular

necrosis of the femoral head) is another cause of lameness in the Yorkshire Terrier, and can be due to failure of the blood supply to the hip during growth. This leads to a painful hip condition and lameness, often at around five months of age. Again, corrective surgery is available and is usually very successful.

Obesity

In a properly fed dog as active as the Yorkshire Terrier, fatness just should not occur, but alas it is all too common. It is usually due to over indulgence with the wrong foods. Do take your veterinarian's advice and do not be afraid of consulting him or her if you think your dog is getting a little plump. After all, obesity can lead to breathing and heart diseases, joint problems and lameness as well as many other unpleasant conditions.

Skin problems

These are not uncommon in the Yorkshire Terrier but most are relatively easily prevented. Puppies should be regularly checked for fleas and lice and one of the very effective sprays or baths, obtainable from your veterinarian, used as necessary. He or she may also advise the use of a preparation around the house to prevent re-infestation.

Mange

Mange can also be a problem. This is due to a tiny mite that burrows in the layers of the skin. There are several forms of mange:
1 Sarcoptic mange can cause scabies in people and causes intense itching both in the dog and the infected owner.
2 Demodectic mange can be particularly difficult to clear up and therefore do consult your veterinarian about any skin problem, especially if there is pruritis (itching) present, no matter how trivial you feel the matter might be.

Mange can only be positively diagnosed on skin scrapings and then treated accordingly.

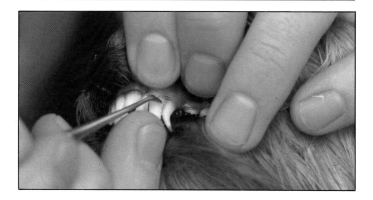

Above: *Plaque and tartar should be removed to avoid the chances of infection. Ask your veterinarian about scaling and other methods.*

Teeth problems

Yorkies do unfortunately have problems with their teeth. Puppies will frequently have erruption problems, the gums will become red and swollen and they will not cut their teeth properly. A 'dog chew' to gnaw often helps.

Double dentition is a very common problem in the Yorkshire Terrier. The deciduous or baby teeth are not shed when the permanent set are fully errupted at about six to nine months old, and so the dog will have a double row of teeth between which food can become lodged and cause serious infection problems. If you are in doubt about the condition, consult your veterinarian.

Calculus (tartar) and *Periodontal disease* are common in the old dog. If there is much build-up of tartar without regular scaling, this will cuase recession of the gums (periodontal disease) and the tooth will loosen and fall out. Many older Yorkies are unfortunately virtually toothless.

Much can be done to preserve the teeth by regular home dental care. Brushing to remove plaque and tartar and reduce infection does help. Special brushes and dog toothpaste are available today. Your veterinarian should be able to advise.

In addition, regular scaling and polishing will help to preserve the teeth. If in doubt, consult the vet.

Worms

Puppies are frequently infested with roundworm, often from their mothers before they are born. The so-called 'pot bellied' and straggle-legged appearance of the traditional wormy puppy is often not seen and frequently evidence of the worms themselves is not apparent. However the veterinarian can detect the presence of worms by a simple faecal test and may request a sample of the animal's stool. Puppies should be regularly wormed every four weeks until they are six months old, particularly for roundworms although tapeworm will affect young animals very occasionally.

From six months onwards, worming with a preparation that covers roundworm, tapeworm and other types of worms makes good sense. Your veterinarian will advise. Today there are very safe and very effective remedies on the market that involve no inconvenience either to owners or animal.

Tapeworms, unlike roundworms, cannot be passed directly from dog to dog but require to pass through an intermediate host. The most common type of tapeworm, Dipylidium caninum, uses the flea as an intermediate host while others can be contracted through eating uncooked meat and offal.

Regular de-worming removes any danger to the dog.

Chapter Four

BREEDING

Basic principles
Mating
Care of the pregnant bitch
Whelping

BASIC PRINCIPLES

All puppies receive 50 per cent of germ plasm from each parent. Without understanding something of the genetic picture of any chosen dog, it is difficult to obtain any specific results in breeding. But by delving into the genetic ancestry of a dog, we are able to evaluate the dog's genetic worth as a whole. Unseen genotype, consisting of pairs of genes for each characteristic — which can be dominant or recessive or one of each (in which case the dominant gene is expressed) — adds up to a pattern of heredity.

We can see the dog's dominant traits as it matures. Good or bad, they are visible. Recessive traits are not always visible. A dominant trait when bred to a dog depicting the same trait will usually breed true and most of the progeny will show this dominant trait. A recessive trait bred to a dog depicting the same trait will result in all offspring exhibiting the recessive trait. A recessive gene cannot be lost; a dominant gene can.

In-breeding
In-breeding is limited to son to mother, father to daughter, half-brother to half-sister and, closest of all, brother to sister.

In-breeding concentrates good features and bad faults. It can strengthen dominants and reveal recessives, giving the breeder control in combining and balancing similar genetic factors. In-breeding is not considered to produce any degeneration; it simply concentrates faults and weaknesses already present, thus enabling the breeder to recognize and eradicate them. It is vitally important when in-breeding to choose animals which are as near perfect as possible. In-breeding creates neither faults nor perfections; it simply fixes them in the progeny.

Line-breeding
This entails the selection of breeding stock which has one or

Right: *A portrait of Champion Ozmilion Dedication, who was awarded the coveted title of Top Dog 1987 in the UK and won Best in Toy Group at Crufts 1988 — a perfect example of line breeding.*

more common ancestor of outstanding worth. This method of breeding has brought the most success in breeding programmes. It is relatively safe. Line breeding to the best individual animals will help to improve the strain.

Outcross breeding
This practice involves the mating of dogs who, in the last five or six generations, are without any common ancestor in their pedigrees.

The novice breeder
I would like to start this chapter with a warning that breeding dogs is not a matter for the novice or pet owner. When you buy a bitch as a pet that is what she should remain, not to become a brood bitch. The welfare and quality of pedigree dogs everywhere should remain in the hands of dedicated and knowledgeable breeders. No novice can hope to assess fully the genetic background of dogs or bitches sold as pets. Therefore, it is quite impossible for pet owners to know, when they mate their bitch to a friend or neighbour's dog, whether such a mating will produce sound and healthy puppies.

Another point to remember is that puppies from three weeks old, until they go to their new owners when they are eight weeks of age, will require much time and attention. They need to be fed at least four times a day. You can be sure that once weaning has commenced the bitch will stop keeping her puppies clean — another chore which you will have to undertake in order to maintain the all-important cleanliness and health of the puppies.

However, if, after these warnings, you particularly wish your bitch to have a litter you

would be wise to consult her breeder who will be able to advise you on a suitable stud dog, and will usually be able to assist with the sale of the puppies.

MATING

The Yorkshire Terrier should never be bred until it is quite mature. Although a bitch will probably have her first season at six or seven months of age, on no account should she be mated at that time. Firstly, she is still a puppy herself and will not be fully developed; secondly, the puppies produced at this early age could be too weak to live. After her second season, providing she is over a year old when it occurs, she can be mated but only — and this is very important — if her weight is at least 5 lbs (2.3 kg).

The bitch's normal mating cycle lasts approximately 21 days. During the first ten days, there is a bright red discharge from the vulva which will gradually fade to pale pink and then to cream. This discharge will last until the 10th or 11th day. From that time until the 18th day, the bitch will normally stand and accept the dog.

Times for mating vary with individual bitches. Some will even accept a stud as early as the fourth day and as late as the 20th day, but the 11th day is usually considered the best.

As soon as the bitch comes into season, you must book an appointment with the owner of the stud dog. A maiden bitch should always be mated to an experienced stud. Two novices can make the mating difficult; it could be prolonged to such an extent that both dog and bitch become quite exhausted.

The 'tie'

Once the dog has mounted the bitch and ejaculation occurs, the dog and the bitch are 'tied'. This occurs when the bitch's vulva constricts the male's engorged penis. The tie can last up to 30 minutes. The reason for the tie is quite unknown, as it is possible for a bitch to conceive without any tie at all. While the tie continues, both dog and bitch should be carefully controlled; a bitch attacking the dog at this time could cause much damage.

When the mating is completed they should be separated. Both can then be given a drink and allowed to relieve themselves and then allowed to rest.

Right: *The Yorkshire Terrier makes a charming pet for both young and old. These two dogs and their young owner are great friends.*

Mating and whelping chart

Jan Mar	Feb Apr	Mar May	Apr June	May Jul	Jun Aug
1 due 5	1 due 5	1 due 3	1 due 3	1 due 3	1 due 3
2 due 6	2 due 6	2 due 4	2 due 4	2 due 4	2 due 4
3 due 7	3 due 7	3 due 5	3 due 5	3 due 5	3 due 5
4 due 8	4 due 8	4 due 6	4 due 6	4 due 6	4 due 6
5 due 9	5 due 9	5 due 7	5 due 7	5 due 7	5 due 7
6 due 10	6 due 10	6 due 8	6 due 8	6 due 8	6 due 8
7 due 11	7 due 11	7 due 9	7 due 9	7 due 9	7 due 9
8 due 12	8 due 12	8 due 10	8 due 10	8 due 10	8 due 10
9 due 13	9 due 13	9 due 11	9 due 11	9 due 11	9 due 11
10 due 14	10 due 14	10 due 12	10 due 12	10 due 12	10 due 12
11 due 15	11 due 15	11 due 13	11 due 13	11 due 13	11 due 13
12 due 16	12 due 16	12 due 14	12 due 14	12 due 14	12 due 14
13 due 17	13 due 17	13 due 15	13 due 15	13 due 15	13 due 15
14 due 18	14 due 18	14 due 16	14 due 16	14 due 16	14 due 16
15 due 19	15 due 19	15 due 17	15 due 17	15 due 17	15 due 17
16 due 20	16 due 20	16 due 18	16 due 18	16 due 18	16 due 18
17 due 21	17 due 21	17 due 19	17 due 19	17 due 19	17 due 19
18 due 22	18 due 22	18 due 20	18 due 20	18 due 20	18 due 20
19 due 23	19 due 23	19 due 21	19 due 21	19 due 21	19 due 21
20 due 24	20 due 24	20 due 22	20 due 22	20 due 22	20 due 22
21 due 25	21 due 25	21 due 23	21 due 23	21 due 23	21 due 23
22 due 26	22 due 26	22 due 24	22 due 24	22 due 24	22 due 24
23 due 27	23 due 27	23 due 25	23 due 25	23 due 25	23 due 25
24 due 28	24 due 28	24 due 26	24 due 26	24 due 26	24 due 26
25 due 29	25 due 29	25 due 27	25 due 27	25 due 27	25 due 27
26 due 30	26 due 30	26 due 28	26 due 28	26 due 28	26 due 28
27 due 31	27 due 1 May	27 due 29	27 due 29	27 due 29	27 due 29
28 due 1 Apr	28 due 2 May	28 due 30	28 due 30	28 due 30	28 due 30
29 due 2 Apr		29 due 31	29 due 1 July	29 due 31	29 due 31
30 due 3 Apr		30 due 1 June	30 due 2 July	30 due 1 Aug	30 due 1 Sep
31 due 4 Apr		31 due 2 June		31 due 2 Aug	

Jul Sep	Aug Oct	Sept Nov	Oct Dec	Nov Jan	Dec Feb
1 due 2	1 due 3	1 due 3	1 due 3	1 due 3	1 due 2
2 due 3	2 due 4	2 due 4	2 due 4	2 due 4	2 due 3
3 due 4	3 due 5	3 due 5	3 due 5	3 due 5	3 due 4
4 due 5	4 due 6	4 due 6	4 due 6	4 due 6	4 due 5
5 due 6	5 due 7	5 due 7	5 due 7	5 due 7	5 due 6
6 due 7	6 due 8	6 due 8	6 due 8	6 due 8	6 due 7
7 due 8	7 due 9	7 due 9	7 due 9	7 due 9	7 due 8
8 due 9	8 due 10	8 due 10	8 due 10	8 due 10	8 due 9
9 due 10	9 due 11	9 due 11	9 due 11	9 due 11	9 due 10
10 due 11	10 due 12	10 due 12	10 due 12	10 due 12	10 due 11
11 due 12	11 due 13	11 due 13	11 due 13	11 due 13	11 due 12
12 due 13	12 due 14	12 due 14	12 due 14	12 due 14	12 due 13
13 due 14	13 due 15	13 due 15	13 due 15	13 due 15	13 due 14
14 due 15	14 due 16	14 due 16	14 due 16	14 due 16	14 due 15
15 due 16	15 due 17	15 due 17	15 due 17	15 due 17	15 due 16
16 due 17	16 due 18	16 due 18	16 due 18	16 due 18	16 due 17
17 due 18	17 due 19	17 due 19	17 due 19	17 due 19	17 due 18
18 due 19	18 due 20	18 due 20	18 due 20	18 due 20	18 due 19
19 due 20	19 due 21	19 due 21	19 due 21	19 due 21	19 due 20
20 due 21	20 due 22	20 due 22	20 due 22	20 due 22	20 due 21
21 due 22	21 due 23	21 due 23	21 due 23	21 due 23	21 due 22
22 due 23	22 due 24	22 due 24	22 due 24	22 due 24	22 due 23
23 due 24	23 due 25	23 due 25	23 due 25	23 due 25	23 due 24
24 due 25	24 due 26	24 due 26	24 due 26	24 due 26	24 due 25
25 due 26	25 due 27	25 due 27	25 due 27	25 due 27	25 due 26
26 due 27	26 due 28	26 due 28	26 due 28	26 due 28	26 due 27
27 due 28	27 due 29	27 due 29	27 due 29	27 due 29	27 due 28
28 due 29	28 due 30	28 due 30	28 due 30	28 due 30	28 due 29
29 due 30	29 due 31	29 due 1 Dec	29 due 31	29 due 31	29 due 2 Mar
30 due 1 Oct	30 due 1 Nov	30 due 2 Dec	30 due 1 Jan	30 due 1 Feb	30 due 3 Mar
31 due 2 Oct	31 due 2 Nov		31 due 2 Jan		31 due 4 Mar

The dog and bitch should be quietly introduced to one another and allowed a little time for courtship play. Soon the bitch will stand and allow the dog to mount and mate her. With a maiden bitch it is often necessary for the owner to hold the bitch's head firmly, making sure she does not snap at the dog.

During the 'tie', which can last between five and forty minutes, the bitch will relax, but care should be taken that neither tries to pull away from the other, causing damage to the dog. Although desirable, a tie is not essential.

CARE OF THE PREGNANT BITCH

Directly after mating, the bitch may be wormed. This can reduce the risk of high infestation of the puppies. Extra food is not essential until the fifth week, when a daily dietary supplement is needed for the foetal development of the puppies. Foods high in protein should be increased and starchy foods decreased. If acceptable, raw beef is especially valuable at this time. Calcium, iron, phosphorus and vitamins should be added to the bitch's food. At this time she should be fed on her own, at the same times each day. Two smaller meals instead of one large helping are more acceptable when she is heavy in whelp. Gentle exercise is necessary, especially during the early weeks of her pregnancy. With a normal size litter it should be possible to tell by the 30th day, with the swelling of the abdomen, that she is in whelp. With a small litter there will be little sign until she is nearer to the time of whelping.

WHELPING

By using the gestation table on pages 60-61, it is possible to prepare for your bitch's whelping well in advance. She should be provided with a whelping box (see below), to which she can become accustomed well before her time. It should preferably be somewhere where her movements can be watched, and also where she can be confined in an enclosure. Otherwise, you may find that she will want to carry the puppies all over the house. We find that bitches at this time usually require and prefer a fairly dark bed which affords protection from other dogs and disturbances. Towards the end of her time, when she is heavy in whelp, she will appreciate

Below: A whelping box —
1 *Removable lid* 2 *Guard rail 2in (5cm) above floor* 3 *Removable front* 4 *Removable base which may be covered by towelling, safely secured underneath* 5 *Hinged lower front* 6 *Feet.*

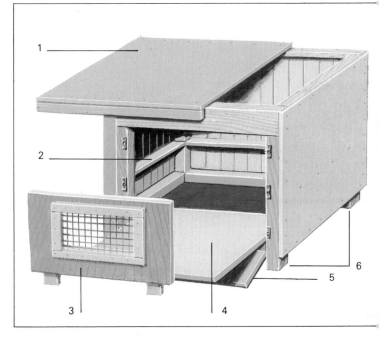

a soft bed to lie on. But as soon as labour commences, all bedding must be removed and the whelping box lined with plenty of newspaper which, as labour commences, she will tear and scratch until it is in shreds. This will help the bitch in labour and is both hygienic and absorbent.

Equipment
A whelping box which should be about 4ft 6in (137cm) square with high sides and back. It should have a front opening and preferably a hinged lid. A guard rail fixed around the three sides of the box will prevent the bitch from accidentally squashing a puppy if it crawls behind her. This rail should consist of wooden battons fastened approximately 2in (5cm) above the floor level.
Several layers of newspaper which can be constantly changed.
Rough towelling, so that if the bitch appears to be tiring, once the puppy is protruding it can be gripped by a piece of towelling and gently drawn out and down, but only when the bitch is straining.
A box with a covered hot water bottle, or electric heating pad on low heat, is necessary to put the first puppies in whilst the bitch is dealing with the newest arrival.
An emergency feeder is necessary in the event that the bitch has no milk. The puppies must be fed with special milk food (milk replacer) strictly according to the directions on the tin.
Glucose should be given to the bitch in her drink during whelping and afterwards.
Disinfectant should be available to use in washing your hands every time before touching the puppies.
Sharp clean scissors and strong cotton for severing the umbilical cord. Bitches usually sever the cord and clean up, but if they are reluctant to do so, this can be done with scissors, making sure that the flow of blood from the placenta (afterbirth) to the puppy has ceased. Nip the cord ¾in (2cm) from the puppy and tie the cord tightly with cotton. On no account

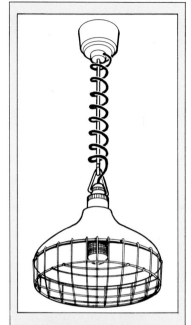

Above: *An infra-red lamp — with a dull emitter and wire guard — which can be raised or lowered to adjust the amount of heat.*

pull away from the puppy; this may cause an umbilical hernia.
Cotton lint for use if the bitch does not release the puppy from its own membranous sac in which it is born. In this case it is necessary to open the sac with your fingers and clean the puppy with the lint or towelling, thereby stimulating it into crying.
An infra red lamp should be suspended over the whelping box. Puppies must have a high temperature at birth, at least 75-80°F (24-27°C).
Or a heating pad which is usually preferred as it allows heat for the puppies without making the bitch uncomfortable. Care must be taken that the flex is well protected and in a position well out of reach of the bitch and puppies.
'Vet beds' are invaluable for keeping the puppies dry. They also give the puppies a firm footing when suckling.

Labour

The commencement of labour in the Yorkie is usually preceded by roughly 24 hours of restlessness and panting accompanied by scratching and tearing up of the paper in her box. This is normally followed by a rather quiet period. Also, at this time the normal temperature of 101.5°F (38.6°C) will drop below 99°F (37.2°C). The labour pains will soon occur, rather far apart to start with but gradually getting closer together in time, continuing until the water bag, looking rather like a small dark brown balloon, appears. Within an hour at the outside the bag will burst, and shortly after this a puppy should appear. Once the bag has burst, if a puppy has not appeared within an hour, it is wise to send for your veterinarian. In the event of labour pains continuing for longer than two hours, or if they appear to be getting weaker, the veterinarian should also be summoned.

Birth

Once the puppy appears the bitch will turn round breaking the sac and biting the navel cord. She will then eat the sac, the cord and the afterbirth. Sometimes the cord, when broken, will leave the afterbirth within the bitch. This will usually be expelled by the birth of the next puppy. The bitch will continue to clean the puppy until the next puppy emerges, when the whole process starts again.

Usually bitches are perfectly capable of whelping the litter without any help from you, but it is better, especially with a maiden bitch (ie having her first litter), for you to be present in case of emergency. Often with the birth of the first puppy the bitch looks quite bemused and it becomes necessary for you to remove the sac. The cord joining the puppy to the afterbirth, once the blood flow has ceased, should be tied tightly with cotton and snipped off between the cotton and the afterbirth. The latter, if not already expelled from the bitch, can then be gently pulled as the bitch strains, until removed.

Remember that you must never pull the cord away from the puppy as this action may cause an umbilical hernia. Always count the number of afterbirths checking against the number of puppies, making sure all have been expelled.

A bitch will often have several puppies in quick succession, then she will rest before the arrival of the last of the litter. During this time a drink of milk with glucose or honey is usually acceptable.

Once the whelping is over the bitch should be allowed to rest quietly without disturbance for several hours, but then she must be allowed out to relieve herself and be quickly returned to her litter. For the first 24 hours give mainly liquid feeds: milk with glucose or honey or a lightly scrambled egg. Water is essential for the bitch's milk supply.

Left: *The water bag at the vulva. This looks like a small, brown balloon. Shortly after the bag bursts, a puppy will be born.*

On the first day after the whelping I strongly advise a visit from your veterinarian when the bitch and her puppies can be examined thoroughly and any abnormalities of the whelps can be diagnosed at once.

When the puppies are between four to six days of age, providing they are strong and healthy, the dew claws must be removed and the tails docked.

Happy and healthy puppies are always quiet and contented. Puppies that cry a lot are either cold or hungry, but constant crying could be a sign of serious trouble and you should call your veterinarian.

Eclampsia

Because of the quick and fatal nature of eclampsia, which can occur at any time but usually between two to three weeks regardless of the number of puppies, it is important to know its cause and symptoms. Eclampsia is caused by lack of calcium in the blood of the nursing bitch. The symptoms are panting, shaking, a somewhat wild expression, a staggering gait, muscular rigidity and restlessness. To save the bitch

Below: *The birth sequence.*
1 The water bag containing the puppy appears at the vulva.
2 The puppy, still encased in the bag, emerges — usually head-first.
3 The bitch tears off the bag and gives the puppy a good wash.
4 The puppy's head is freed first so it can take its first breath.

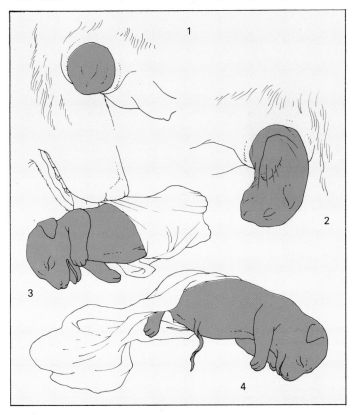

it is vital that veterinary assistance is sought immediately for an intravenous injection of calcium.

Weaning

When the puppies' eyes are open, between 10-16 days, they will soon be moving around learning to walk. From this time get them accustomed to the sound of your voice and to being handled.

At approximately four weeks of age their milk teeth, 28 in all, will begin to erupt, and although they will still be getting plenty of milk from the bitch, now is the time to start weaning. A little scraped raw beef, about 4oz (113.5g), fed to them with your fingers, is in my opinion the quickest method. Puppies first suck the meat and once tasted attack the remainder with relish. Quite soon, after a few days, they will be eating two meat meals a day. Once the puppies are eating the meat easily, they should be introduced to a warm milk meal. This may be cows' milk or goats' milk, which is excellent.

Alternatively, you can use a well-known brand of puppy weaning food which I have found very satisfactory; the puppies like it and it is easy to prepare. The milk may be mixed with a cereal such as corn flakes or oats made into

Above: *A proud mother with her litter of puppies at two weeks of age. As you can see, all Yorkie puppies are born black.*

recedes, will quite often regurgitate her food if allowed near the puppies. Providing she has not eaten any large lumps of meat or biscuit, this will do no harm but will necessitate feeding the bitch again. It is wiser to keep the bitch away from her puppies for at least an hour after she has eaten.

Once the puppies are completely weaned they should be fed from separate dishes enabling you to know how much each puppy consumes and to check that all are eating well. Quantities will vary with the size and appetite of each puppy. Feed about every four hours, two meals of meat with a little moistened puppy meal, two of cereal moistened with milk or broth. All food should be fresh and minced or chopped finely.

Puppy development
Weight A puppy should have doubled its birth weight by eight days of age.
Sucking reflex In healthy puppies this is strong at birth. It will be weak if the puppy is abnormal, cold or premature.
Body temperature This is approximately 94-99°F (34.4-37.2°C) in the first two weeks and 97-100°F (36.1-37.7°C) from two to four weeks. The normal temperature of an adult dog is 101.5°F (38.6°C). This is why it is essential to keep the puppies very warm. The shivering reflex does not develop until approximately eight days after birth. Therefore, during the first two weeks of life, the temperature in the whelping box should be high — at least 75-80°F (23.8-26.6°C). Normal puppies have a twitching action between one to three weeks. This disappears after they are a month old.
Locomotion Puppies can stand at three weeks, walk and run at four weeks.
Eyes These open between 10 and 16 days; at this time it is essential to protect them against strong light.
Ears These open at approximately 13 days of age. At four weeks, but rarely before, the puppies will recognise their owner.

porridge. Once or twice a week, scrambled egg makes a nice change. As the puppies mature well, toasted wholemeal bread can be added to both meat and milk meals.

During this weaning period the mother should be separated from her puppies for longer and longer periods. There is a natural instinct, which can cause distress to the owner: the bitch, as her milk

Above: *Although this Yorkshire Terrier puppy is still very young, the coat markings are already clearly discernible.*

Below: *These four young littermates snuggle up close to one another away from their nest; it is crucial to keep them very warm.*

Left: *The eyes of these two week-old Yorkie puppies are just beginning to open. It is vital, at this stage in their development, to protect the puppies from strong or direct light.*

Right: *This young puppy already displays good characteristics of the Yorkshire Terrier breed — well set ears and clear tan markings. Puppies will be able to stand at three weeks and walk at four.*

Below: *This young bitch (of Verolian breeding) is just 12 weeks of age, but already she shows great promise for the show ring — alert, bright-eyed with a clearing of the black coat.*

Chapter Five

GROOMING

The pet Yorkie
Techniques past and present
Bathing the show or pet Yorkie
Show preparation of the topknot
The show Yorkie

The pet Yorkie

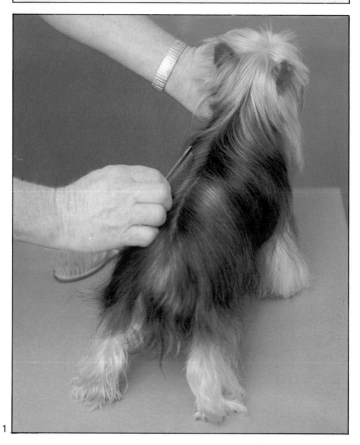

1 Begin the pet Yorkie's daily grooming by combing through the body coat using a steel comb with half wide and half fine teeth.

2 Use the wide teeth of the comb to groom the backs of ears and to remove any mats or knots caused by romping with playmates.

3

3 *The wide teeth are also used to comb out face furnishings and beard of an older Yorkie. Finish off with the fine end of the comb.*

4 *The daily grooming of the pet Yorkie is nearly over. Finish off by making a parting along the back using a pure bristle brush.*

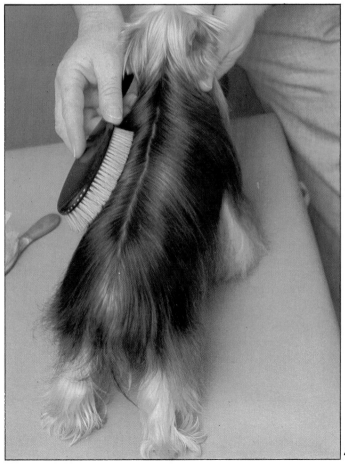

4

Grooming techniques, 1895

This article from the canine paper, Dogs, *published in England in 1895, makes interesting and amusing reading in a comparison with the grooming of Yorkies today.*

Dogs Up To Date
The Yorkshire Terrier

'This variety is unquestionably one of the most beautiful of any breed of dog, but is rarely seen in perfection except at shows, as the attention that has to be bestowed upon its toilet renders the Yorkshireman a somewhat exacting pet. Nor is it adapted for much outdoor work, as its silky coat is ill-suited to keep off cold or rain.

'The Yorkshire Terrier, beautiful as his variety is, can scarcely be recommended to beginners as a pet. As suggested above, the luxuriance and condition of his coat necessitate the constant attention of an experienced attendant and, unless the jacket is properly treated, there will be little but disappointment in store for his owner. The best shown specimens of the breed pass a considerable portion of their time "in pickle", by which it is understood that their coats are smeared over with some nostrums which their owners believe, and no doubt with some reason, add to the growth and silkiness of their hair. The ingredients which compose these dressings for the coats are usually regarded in the light of the most sacred secrets, which each owner jealously guards, lest some opposition breeder should profit by his experience. There is very little doubt, however, that cocoa-nut oil forms a considerable proportion of many of the recipes, and under any circumstances it can be

Below: *An example of one of the many stylish pet trims available for the Yorkie. Consult a professional dog groomer.*

Right: *A rather different style of pet trim for easy care where the body coat has been trimmed short and the head scissored.*

recommended as an excellent dressing for the jackets of long and silky coated breeds.

'As the necessity for applying some oily substance to the coats of Yorkshire Terriers is unavoidable, these little dogs pass a good deal of their time in specially constructed boxes with immovable plate-glass fronts, the door being at the back, whilst ventilation is secured by holes which are bored high up on either side. The Terriers can scarcely be allowed full liberty whilst they are in pickle as, in the first place, their greasy jackets would spoil everything they came in contact with, and, secondly, the application of the oily compound to their hair and skin has the effect of making them feel very cold unless extra precautions are taken to ensure their warmth. In spite, however, of the above circumstances combining to make the Yorkshire Terrier one of the most difficult of all breeds to keep in good condition, the variety is a most engaging one. The Yorkshireman is a very sharp, vivacious little dog, and always on the alert. He does not make friends with everybody, but is devoted to his mistress or master; and, therefore, if the beginner is not too anxious to possess a specimen with a very luxuriant coat, and is content to own a really handsome little animal, he might do far worse than invest in a specimen of the breed as an indoor companion. These, if properly looked after, will be very handsome, and will develop fairly long coats. But, in order to avoid disappointment, the owners of such animals must not expect them to win prizes in strong competition at the leading shows, at which the length of their jackets is a very important factor.'

——— **Bathing the show or pet Yorkie** ———

1

1 *Carefully remove any crackers (see page 89) from the body and head. The coat is quite oily, so first comb the hair thoroughly.*

2 *Test the water temperature and place the dog on a mat. Always remember to wash your brush and comb to remove dirt or grease.*

2

3

3 *After inserting cotton wool in the ears, wet head and furnishings avoiding eyes. Next wash the short hairs on the inside and outside of the ears using a small bristle brush to remove any oil residue applied to show coat (page 87).*

4 *First, shampoo the dog's head. Always use a mild 'tearless' shampoo but still take care not to get in the eyes. Next, shampoo the body using an insecticidal shampoo working down the hair shaft.*

5 *Carefully, rinse the head and body of your Yorkshire Terrier. Note how the dog in this photograph is being gently held by its owner under the body whilst the spray is used along the back.*

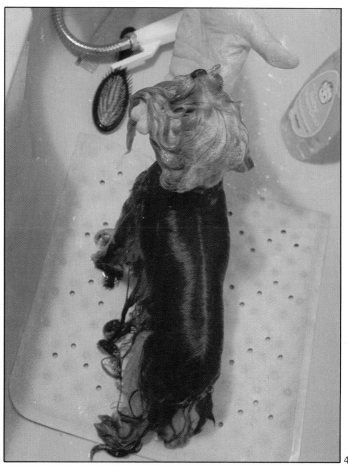

4

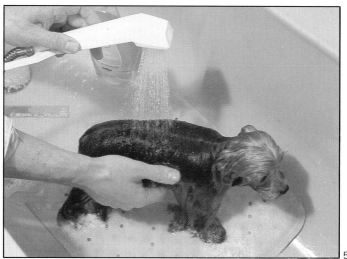

5

6

6 *It is very important to rinse thoroughly to remove all traces of shampoo from the coat. Remember to rinse under the body as well.*

7 *Now, apply a mild conditioner to the coat to prevent the hair from becoming tangled or knotted. Work in the conditioner down the hair.*

7

8 *After another thorough rinsing to remove the conditioner, remove excess water by gently squeezing the hair downwards as shown.*

9 *When you have removed the excess water by hand, wrap the dog in a warm and dry towel to absorb moisture.*

8

9

10 *This beautiful little Yorkie, with its full show coat freshly bathed, i. now ready for the next stage — combing and blow-drying.*

11 *Before you begin blow-drying, comb through the coat starting at the ends of the hair gradually working upwards the roots.*

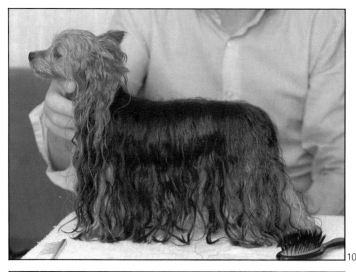

10

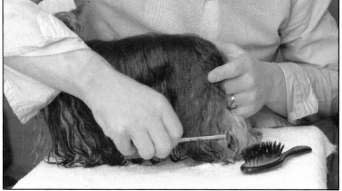

11

12

12 *After the whole coat has been thoroughly combed, begin blow-drying at medium temperature using a soft bristle brush as shown.*

13 *Blow-dry the body coat completely so that it is quite straight and smooth, but leaving head and furnishings damp.*

13

14

14 *Now dry the furnishings as shown, brushing down the hair with the pure bristle brush while directing the dryer downwards.*

15 *Complete the drying process by blow-drying the topknot. Direct the flow of hot air on to the hair as you brush it backwards over the head away from the face.*

16 *The photograph shows a sideview of the correct position of the parting of the topknot and furnishings, ie in a straight line from the ear to the eye.*

15

Show preparation of the topknot

16

17

17 *The correct parting of the topknot and furnishings across the back of the head — in a straight line from ear to ear.*

18 *Having made the correct partings, the topknot hair is gathered up and secured with a small, strong rubber band.*

18

19 *Now, trim away any excess hair from the ears with small electric clippers, as shown, or use a pair of small, sharp scissors.*

20 *Only a bow is required for the topknot to complete this beautiful picture. The dog has the correct tan shading and ear carriage.*

19

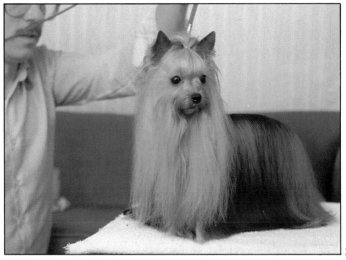

20

The show Yorkie

21

21 *To prevent damage to the coat, socks are placed on the feet and the ends of the hair oiled with the dog lying on its back.*

22 *For the socks, use a finger bandage with an applicator as seen in the photograph. Hold the foot gently while fitting the sock.*

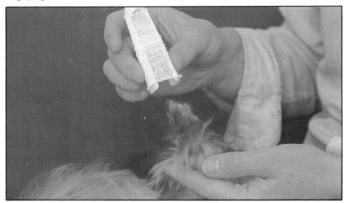

22

23

23 *Place the bandage, complete with applicator, over the Yorkie's foot and with one hand hold the bottom of the bandage to the foot.*

24 *Keeping hold of the bandage over the foot, remove applicator halfway from bandage and then twist the bandage as shown.*

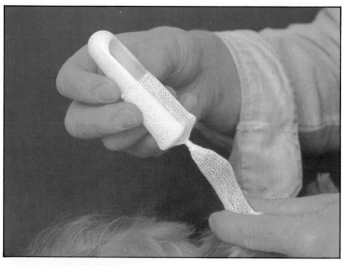

24

25

25 *Remove the applicator from the upper half of the bandage and turn back over the foot. Secure the sock with a strip of plaster.*

26 *The finished sock looking neat and comfortable for the dog to wear. Socks prevent the dog scratching at crackers (see pages 88-91) and damaging the coat.*

27 *With the dog still on its back, dip a soft bristle brush in oil (preferably almond) and brush through the ends of the hair to help prevent it from breaking.*

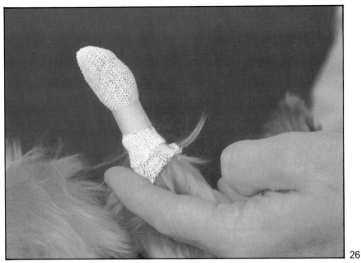

26

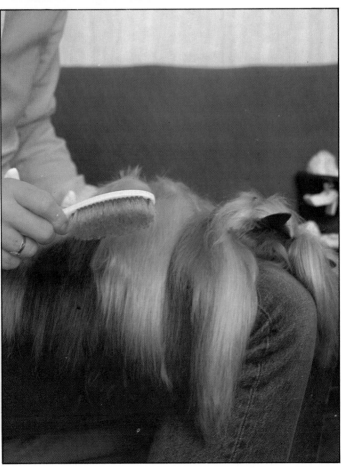

27

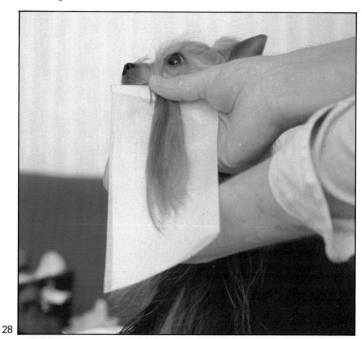

28

28 *Crackering begins with the face furnishings. Place a section of the hair, ie the moustache, on a piece of acid-free paper.*

29 *Carefully fold both sides of the paper over the section of hair, as shown, and hold the strip out straight, away from the face.*

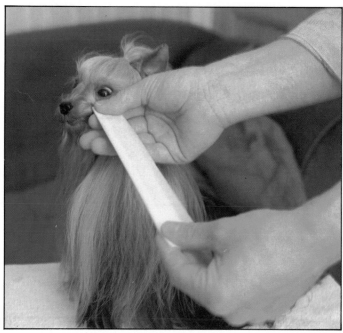

29

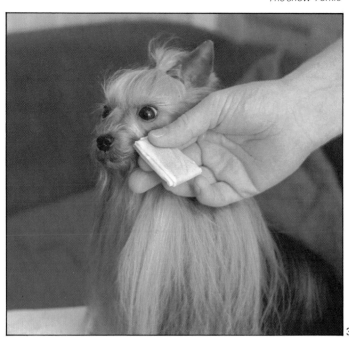

30

30 *Bring the bottom of the strip up to meet the top and fold. Then fold the strip in half once again to complete the cracker.*

31 *Secure the packet of hair in place with a strong rubber band. The result is a safe and neat cracker, as you can see.*

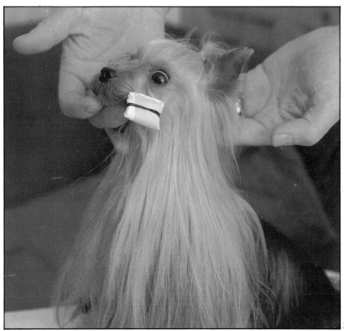

31

32

32 *Repeat the crackering process on the other side of the moustache. Then wrap and fold the beard in the same way, as shown.*

33 *Here you can see the Yorkie's head complete with crackers on the moustache and beard. The crackers look tidy and secure.*

33

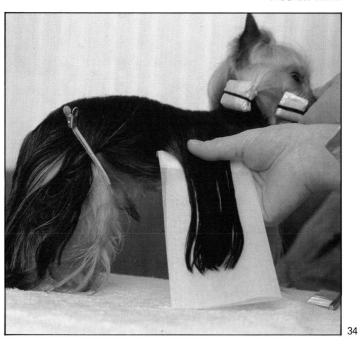

34

34 *Now continue crackering the ear furnishings, tail and body. Part the body coat into sections as shown in the photograph.*

35 *The completed crackering of the face, ear furnishings, body coat chest and tail. The legs are usually crackered also.*

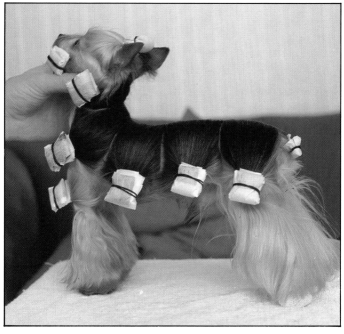

35

Chapter Six

SHOWING

The Breed Standards
Choosing a potential show puppy
Training and preparation for exhibition
The show systems
Your first show

THE BREED STANDARDS

The breed standard endeavours to describe in words an ideal specimen of the breed to provide a basis for assessment in the show ring. As a word picture, however, it is subject to many different interpretations by judges and exhibitors.

The UK standard
This is reproduced by kind permission of the Kennel Club.
General appearance Long coated, coat hanging quite straight and evenly down each side, a parting extending from nose to end of tail. Very compact and neat, carriage very upright conveying an important air. General outline conveying impression of vigorous and well-proportioned body.
Characteristics Alert, intelligent toy terrier.
Temperament Spirited with even disposition.
Head and skull Rather small and flat, not too prominent or round in skull, not too long in muzzle, black nose.
Eyes Medium, dark, sparkling, with

Below: *The diagram illustrates the skeletal parts of the Yorkshire Terrier, together with the conformation points referred to in the Breed Standards.*

Skeleton
1 Skull 2 Cervical vertebra
3 Thoracic vertebra 4 Rib 5 Lumber vertebra 6 Coccygeal vertebra
7 Pelvis 8 Femur 9 Patella 10 Fibula
11 Metatarsus 12 Tarsus 13 Tibia
14 Sternum 15 Phalanges 16 Radius
17 Ulna 18 Humerus 19 Scapula
Conformation points
A Occiput B Forehead C Stop
D Muzzle E Shoulder F Elbow
G Forearm H Pastern I Hock
J Stifle K Thigh L Loin M Tail
N Back O Withers

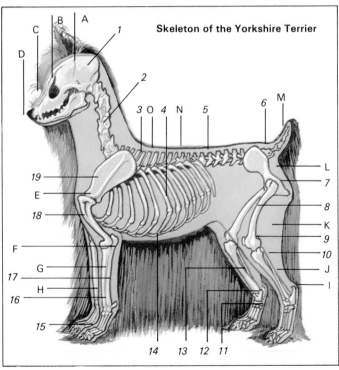

Skeleton of the Yorkshire Terrier

sharp intelligent expression and placed to look directly forward. Not prominent. Edge of eyelids dark.

Ears Small, V-shaped, carried erect, not too far apart, covered with short hair, colour very deep, rich tan.

Mouth Perfect, regular and complete scissor bite, i.e. the upper teeth closely overlapping the lower teeth and set square to the jaws. Teeth well placed with even jaws.

Neck Good reach.

Forequarters Well laid shoulders, legs straight, well covered with hair of rich golden tan a few shades lighter at ends than at roots, not extending higher on forelegs than elbow.

Body Compact with moderate spring of rib, good loin. Level back.

Hindquarters Legs quite straight when viewed from behind, moderate turn of stifle. Well covered with hair of rich golden tan a few shades lighter at ends than at roots, not extending higher on hindlegs than stifle.

Feet Round; nails black.

Tail Customarily docked to medium length with plenty of hair, darker blue in colour than rest of body, especially at end of tail. Carried a little higher than level of back.

Gait/movement Free with drive; straight action front and behind, retaining level topline.

Coat Hair on body moderately long, perfectly straight (not wavy), glossy; fine silky texture, not woolly. Fall on head long, rich golden tan, deeper in colour at sides of head, about ear roots and on muzzle where it should be very long. Tan on head not to extend on to neck, nor must any sooty or dark hair intermingle with any of tan.

Colour Dark steel blue (not silver blue), extending from occiput to root of tail, never mingled with fawn, bronze or dark hairs. Hair on chest rich, bright tan. All tan hair darker at the roots than in middle, shading to still lighter at tips.

Size Weight up to 7 lbs (3.1 kg).

Faults Any departure from the foregoing points should be considered a fault and the seriousness with which the fault

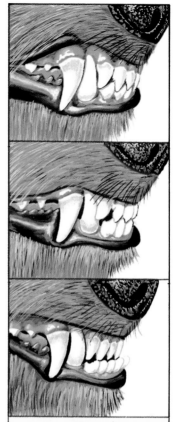

Bites

The top diagram shows the correct 'scissor' bite; the top teeth fit over the bottom teeth. The middle shows the incorrect 'level' bite where the front teeth meet top to top. The diagram above shows the 'undershot' mouth. This is also an incorrect bite. In this case, the lower teeth come in front of the top teeth.

should be regarded should be in exact proportion to its degree.

Note: Male animals should have two apparently normal testicles fully descended into the scrotum.

Notes on the standard

1 The Yorkie is a compact, solid, small dog with good head carriage and reach of neck, level topline, with a tail carried slightly higher than the back.

2 The body should be compact and well proportioned.

3 Front legs should be quite straight. The hindquarters when seen from behind are straight, never bowed.

4 Feet are round like a cat's paw.

5 The coat should be fine, silky and glossy in texture, quite thick, hanging quite straight without any curl or wave, never woolly. The tan should be rich and golden. Tan on head must not extend onto neck, or above the elbows on forequarters, or the stifle joints on the hindquarters. Hair on body should be a clear dark steel blue.

The US standard
General appearance That of a long-haired toy terrier whose blue and tan coat is parted on the face and from the base of the skull to the end of the tail and hangs evenly and quite straight down each side of body. The body is neat, compact and well proportioned. The dog's high head carriage and confident manner should give the appearance of vigor and self-importance.

Head Small and rather flat on top, the skull not too prominent or round, the muzzle not too long, with the bite neither undershot nor overshot and teeth sound. Either scissors bite or level bite is acceptable. The nose is black. Eyes are medium in size and not too prominent; dark in color and sparkling with a sharp, intelligent expression. Eye rims are dark. Ears are small, V-shaped, carried erect and set not too far apart.

Body Well proportioned and very compact. The back is rather short, the back line level, with height at shoulder the same as at the rump.

Above right: *The Breed Standards specify V-shaped ears; this Yorkie's ear is too rounded.*

Right: *Another ear fault. The Breed Standards call for a small ear in the Yorkshire Terrier; these are too large.*

Below: *The ears of this Yorkshire Terrier are too far apart for exhibition in the show ring. This is a show fault.*

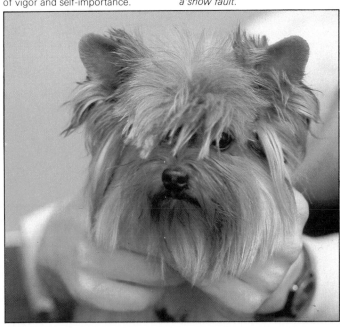

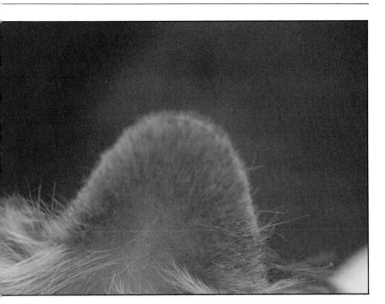

Above: *This Yorkshire Terrier in pet trim slopes down at the withers so that the back is not level — a bad fault.*

Above right: *This is another pet Yorkie with three bad faults: lack of neck, a roached back (arched) and a low tail set.*

Legs and feet Forelegs should be straight, elbows neither in nor out. Hind legs straight when viewed from behind, but stifles are moderately bent when viewed from the sides. Feet are round with black toenails. Dewclaws, if any, are generally removed from the hind legs. Dewclaws on the forelegs may be removed.

Tail Docked to a medium length and carried slightly higher than the level of the back.

Coat Quality, texture and quantity of coat are of prime importance. Hair is glossy, fine and silky in texture. Coat on the body is moderately long and perfectly straight (not wavy). It may be trimmed to floor length to give ease of movement and a neater appearance, if desired. The fall on the head is long, tied with one bow in center of head or parted in the middle and tied with two bows. Hair on muzzle is very long. Hair should be trimmed short on tips of ears and may be trimmed on feet to give them a neat appearance.

Colors Puppies are born black and tan and are normally darker in body color, showing an intermingling of black hair in the tan until they are matured. Color of hair

Right: *The tan on the forequarter must not go higher than the elbows. On the hindlegs it must not go higher than the stifle.*

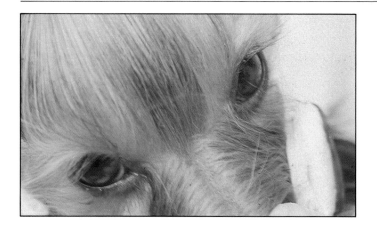

Early breed standards

An exhibition of sporting and other dogs, held under Kennel Club rules at Aston lower grounds in England on 5, 7 and 8 May 1883, produced one of the first descriptions of the breed to be printed in a catalogue. The judge on the day, a Mr J W Berrie, also wrote the following under the class heading of Yorkshire Terriers:

'Head small; eyes bright and keen; legs and feet straight and strong; general appearance compact; coat on body, tail and head should be abundant and as long, straight and silky as possible; colour light blue on head and dark slate on body.'

Five dogs were entered. First prize went to Mrs Foster's Bradford Hero (see Chapter One); second prize to Mrs Troughear's Lancashire Lad, Spinkwell Ben (sired by Huddersfield Ben).

Although the breed standard was not referred to in the second edition of *Stonehenge*, published 1872, in the fourth edition of 1887 the following standard and 'Points in Judging' were included. This is the same standard as reproduced in the sixth edition of Gordon Stables', *'Our Friend the Dog'* first published in 1883. In both books, the Yorkshire Terrier Club is credited with the formation of the standard at least 11 years before the official foundation of the Yorkshire Terrier Club in England in 1898.

The Standard 1987

'The general appearance should be that of a long-coated pet dog, the coat hanging quite straight and evenly down each side, a parting extending from the nose to the end of the tail. The animal should be very compact and neat, the carriage being very sprightly, bearing an important air. Although the frame is hidden beneath a mantle of hair, the general outline should be such as to suggest the existence of a vigorous and well-proportioned body.

Head should be rather small and flat, not too prominent or round in the skull; rather broad at the muzzle, with a perfectly black nose; the hair on the muzzle very long, which should be a rich, deep tan, not sooty or grey. Under the chin long hair, and about the same colour as the centre of the head, which should be a bright, golden tan, and not on any account intermingled with dark or sooty hairs. Hair on the sides of the head should be very long, and a few shades deeper tan than the centre of the head, especially about the ear-roots.

Eyes Medium in size, dark in colour; having a sharp, intelligent expression, and placed so as to look directly forward. They should not be prominent; the edges of the eyelids should also be of a dark colour.

Left: A close-up of a Yorkshire Terrier's head to illustrate the required transitiion in colouring from dark to golden tan.

on body and richness of tan on head and legs are of prime importance in adult dogs, to which the following color requirements apply:

Blue Is a dark steel-blue, not a silver-blue and not mingled with fawn, bronzy or black hairs.

Tan All tan hair is darker at the roots than in the middle, shading to still lighter tan at the tips. There

should be no sooty or black hair intermingled with any of the tan.

Color on body The blue extends over the body from back of neck to root of tail. Hair on tail is a darker blue, especially at end of tail.

Headfall A rich golden tan, deeper in color at sides of head, at ear roots and on the muzzle, with ears a deep rich tan. Tan color should not extend down on back of neck.

Chest and legs A bright, rich tan, not extending above the elbow on the forelegs nor above the stifle on the hind legs.

Weight Must not exceed seven pounds *(3.2kg)*.

Ears Cut or uncut; if cut, quite erect; if uncut, to be small, V-shaped, and carried semi-erect, covered with short hair. Colour to be a deep dark tan.

Mouth Good even mouth; teeth as sound as possible. A dog having lost a tooth or two, through accident or otherwise, not the least objectionable, providing the jaws are even.

Body Very compact and a good loin, and level on the top of the back.

Coat The hair as long and straight as possible (not wavy), which should be glossy like silk (not woolly), extending from the back of the head to the root of the tail. Colour a bright steel blue, and on no account intermingled the least with fawn, light, or dark hairs.

Legs Quite straight, which should be of a bright golden tan, and well covered with hair, a few shades lighter at the ends than at roots.

Feet As round as possible; toe nails black.

Weight Divided into two classes, viz, under 5 lbs and over 5 lbs *(2.3kg)* but not to exceed 12 lbs *(5.4kg)*.'

*This table of points, although now officially disallowed by the Kennel Club in the UK, is still occasionally referred to by both breeders and many judges.

Points in Judging

	value
Quantity and colour of hair on back	25
Quality of coat	15
Tan	15
Head	10
Eyes	5
Mouth	5
Ears	5
Legs and feet	5
Body and general appearance	10
Tail	5
Total	100

A slightly different standard was reproduced in the late Theo Marples' book, *Show Dogs* published in 1916. This remained in force in the UK until the publication of a new standard by the Kennel Club in 1987. The 'Value of Points' was, however, somewhat altered as follows:

Value of Points*

Formation and Terrier appearance	15
Colour of hair on body	15
Richness of tan on head and legs	15
Quality and texture of coat	10
Quantity and length of coat	10
Head	10
Mouth	5
Legs and feet	5
Ears	5
Eyes	5
Tail (carriage of)	5
Total	100

CHOOSING A POTENTIAL SHOW PUPPY

It is quite impossible to buy a puppy of eight to ten weeks that can be guaranteed as show quality. No breeder of repute would sell a Yorkie as a show specimen before it had reached at least six months of age, when it is possible to ascertain its real show potential. Several changes occur between five to seven months of age: the second teeth appear, so that the 'bite' will be determined (the 'scissor' bite is required for showing — see page 00). The overall shape of the dog will be more or less established as will be the texture of the coat which should be very fine, silky,

fairly thick and long; never coarse, wiry, woolly or curly. Coat colour at this age should be black, although the change from black to dark steel blue can occur from three months. If the change starts this early, the final colour is often a pale silver blue. To achieve the desired steel blue, it is considered that the break in colour should occur between eight and ten months. Tan on the head, legs and under the tail should be clear and bright. The skull should be fairly flat between the ears and not too long in the muzzle. Ears should be carried erect and not too wide apart. Eyes should be of medium size, dark and expressive; the nose and eye-rims black. The topline should be level; the legs should move straight. The back is

short; the general overall appearance being of a square dog.

Before purchasing a show puppy read everything about the breed. Visit several shows, taking note of the puppy classes in particular. Talk to the breeders — their advice is always forthcoming. Be sure to study the breed standard, but no dog of any breed is perfect.

Left: *A charming study of a 12 week-old bitch of show quality. Note the well-shaped ears and dark, expressive eyes.*

Below: *This photograph illustrates much of the charm and beauty of the breed and the rich golden tan of the topknot and fall.*

TRAINING AND PREPARATION FOR EXHIBITION

In my opinion, the presentation for the show ring of the Yorkshire Terrier requires more skill and dedication than any other breed. From a very young age, in fact as soon as the hair is long enough, early wrapping of the hair to protect and promote growth is essential. The topknot and whiskers are usually the first to be wrapped (see Chapter Five on Grooming). As soon as this occurs, the puppy must be under constant supervision as he may try to chew or scratch the crackers. The younger the dog is when you start crackering, the sooner it will accept the fully crackered coat. Needless to say it must not be allowed to play with other puppies who would easily damage the coat.

The show position

As Yorkies are always shown on boxes and are required to stand and pose in the correct position, it is necessary that the dog is trained to accept the box and to stand in a show position until the judge has made his or her final placings. I have found that it is much easier to start this training from a very young age, even at seven to eight weeks of age, making the lesson very short to start with — no more than a minute every day. Always reward the dog with much praise and a tit-bit of something it particularly enjoys.

The judge's examination

Once the dog is used to standing well on the box, it must now be trained to stand on a table and become accustomed to the various ways judges carry out their examination. Get all your friends and visitors to run their hands over

the dog, making sure they examine the teeth by gently parting the lips with one hand placed on the lower jaw and the other on the top jaw. The judge then raises the upper lip and lowers the bottom lip which is all that is required to check the Yorkie's bite and number of teeth.

The 'triangle'
Most judges require dogs to move in a triangle. To train your Yorkie to move in a triangle on your left side, it is a good idea to set up a temporary ring. Get a friend to act as the 'judge' while you move in a triangle, always keeping the dog between you and the judge. Then move straight up and down the 'ring' away from and towards the judge. When doing so, do not turn abruptly, just move round in a small 'U' turn without breaking the dog's stride. If you turn too quickly, it can lose its stride and will move badly on its return to the judge. Always encourage the dog with your voice and praise it when it walks well.

SHOW SYSTEMS

Having prepared and trained your Yorkie for its first outing into the exciting world of dog shows, you will need to study the whole range of shows available to you and their various entry requirements. Dog shows are run under the auspices of national kennel clubs, and the nature of the shows themselves and

Below left: *It is wise to start crackering early to avoid resistance. This youngster is in the early head crackers.*

Below: *Early training on the box to assume the correct show stance — and maintain it — is essential for the potential show Yorkie.*

the rules and regulations governing them vary in a number of aspects from country to country (addresses of kennel clubs listed in the Appendix).

The groups

Some shows are specific to one breed (or variety of breed), called specialty shows; others encompass all breeds. At the All-Breed or Championship shows, once the Best of Breed has been awarded for each individual breed competing in the show, these winners must compete in their 'group' before they can be considered for the top award, Best in Show. In the UK, all breeds are divided into six groups, with the Yorkshire being a member of the Toy group. In the US, where the group system of judging is also used, all breeds are divided into seven groups. As in the UK, the Yorkshire Terrier is included in the Toy group.

Below: *Training at home to move your young Yorkie in a triangle on your left side is invaluable when you start exhibiting.*

Registration

In order to exhibit your dog at any show run under the jurisdiction of the Kennel Club, your puppy must be registered at the KC. You will have been given by the breeder one of two forms: a pink form entitled 'Application to Register One Dog'; or a white and green form, 'The Registration Certificate'. In the first case, you will need to fill in the necessary particulars and choose a suitable name for your puppy. In the latter case, the puppy will have already been named by the breeder but needs to be transferred from the breeder into your own name. In both cases, the forms must be signed by you and sent with the appropriate fee to the Kennel Club.

Types of show

The various types of show in the UK are detailed below. It would be wise for a novice exhibitor with a young dog to choose a local or small show, graduating to the larger Open and Championship shows as the puppy matures.

Exemption Show This is usually held in aid of a charitable cause and is the only dog show where unregistered dogs may be exhibited. These are usually carefree and informal occasions held more for fun than serious competition, and as they always have four classes for pedigree dogs, often including a puppy class, this

Above: *The Yorkie box with its cover, used for exhibiting in the show ring, which usually has pockets for brush and comb.*

is an ideal show for a puppy's first outing.

Sanction Show This is confined to members of the canine club or association holding the show. Once again, if you are a member of a club, they are great shows for puppies.

Primary Show This is very similar to a Sanction Show, again restricted to breed club members and also excellent for puppies.

Limited Show This is restricted to members of clubs or societies or to exhibitors within a specified, geographic area.

Open Shows These are usually fairly large shows which are open to all exhibitors but without any Challenge Certificates on offer.

Championship Shows These are the most important events in the dog show calendar. At these shows, the Kennel Club Challenge Certificates are on offer. The number of CCs allocated to a breed are based on the annual number of dogs registered at the Kennel Club. Hence, the numerically larger breeds are awarded more CCs in the year than their less popular counterparts.

Awards

Challenge Certificate (CC) This is awarded to the Best Dog and Best

Bitch in each breed, but only when, as is stated on the Certificate given to the owner and signed by the judge, 'in his opinion the dog is worthy of the title of Champion'. A judge not of this opinion can still award Best of Sex (Dog or Bitch) but must withold the CC.

Reserve Challenge Certificate This is awarded to the Reserve Best of Sex. If the CC winner is disqualified, the Reserve Best of Sex is awarded the CC.

Champion A dog attains the title of Champion when it has won all three CCs at three Championship Shows under three different judges providing one CC is awarded when the dog is over 12 months old. All judges, before being passed to award these Certificates, are assessed by the Kennel Club for their experience, knowledge and achievements in the breed they are to judge.

Junior Warrant This may be awarded, by application to the Kennel Club, for any dog which has amassed 25 points in breed classes before the age of 18 months. Points are awarded as follows: one point for a first prize at an Open Show, and three points awarded for a first prize at a Championship show where Challenge Certificates are on offer for the breed.

Above: *A Yorkshire Terrier moving well in the show ring at one of the Championship Shows in the UK on a lovely summer's day.*

Classes
The following is a definition of classes held at Open and Championship shows, taken from the Kennel Club Regulations for the Definition of Classes (reproduced by kind permission of the Kennel Club). These regulations are printed in all show schedules and should be studied carefully before entering your dog in any show. The term 'dog' in this context applies to both dogs and bitches. At most Championship Shows, classes are duplicated for each sex, ie Puppy Dog, Puppy Bitch, etc. At the Open and smaller shows, these classes are usually mixed with dogs and bitches judged in the same class.

Minor puppy For dogs of six and not exceeding nine calendar months of age on the first day of the show.

Puppy For dogs of six and not exceeding twelve calendar months of age on the first day of the show.

Junior For dogs of six and not exceeding 18 calendar months of age on the first day of the show.

Maiden For dogs which have not

Above: *Osman Sameja with Champion Ozmilion Dedication winning the Toy Group at Crufts Dog Show in London in 1988.*

won a Challenge Certificate or a First Prize at an Open or Championship Show (Puppy, Special Puppy, Minor Puppy and Special Minor Puppy classes excepted).

Novice For dogs which have not won a Challenge Certificate or three or more First Prizes at Open and Championship Shows (Puppy, Special Puppy, Minor Puppy and Special Minor Puppy classes excepted).

Tyro For dogs which have not won a Challenge Certificate or five or more First Prizes at Open and Championship Shows (Puppy, Special Puppy, Minor Puppy and Special Minor Puppy classes excepted).

Debutant For dogs which have not won a Challenge Certificate or a First Prize at a Championship Show (Puppy, Special Puppy, Minor Puppy and Special Minor Puppy classes excepted).

Undergraduate For dogs which have not won a Challenge Certificate or three or more First Prizes at Championship Shows

(Puppy, Special Puppy, Minor Puppy and Special Minor Puppy classes excepted).

Graduate For dogs which have not won a Challenge Certificate or four or more First Prizes at Championship Shows in Graduate, Post Graduate, Minor Limit, Mid Limit, Limit and Open Classes, whether restricted or not.

Minor Limit For dogs which have not won two Challenge Certificates or three or more First Prizes in all at Championship Shows in Minor Limit, Mid Limit, Limit and Open Classes, confined to the breed, whether restricted or not, at shows where Challenge Certificates were offered for the breed.

Mid Limit For dogs which have not won three Challenge Certificates or five or more First Prizes in all at Championship Shows in Mid Limit, Limit and Open Classes, confined to the breed, whether restricted or not, at shows where CCs were offered for the breed.

Limit For dogs which have not won three Challenge Certificates under three different judges or seven or more First Prizes in all, at Championship Shows in Limit and Open Classes, confined to the breed, whether restricted or not, at shows where Challenge Certificates were offered for the breed.

Open For all dogs of the breeds for which the class is provided and eligible for entry at the show.

In addition, there are Veteran classes for dogs over five years of age, Brace and Team classes for pairs and teams of dogs, and sweepstake classes, open to Veteran, Brace, Team, Stud Dog, Brood Bitch and Breeders Classes, in which some of the fees may be awarded as prize money.

Forthcoming shows

The two weekly dog papers available in the UK, *Our Dogs* and *Dog World*, carry a comprehensive list of all forthcoming shows, giving the venue, date, type of show with the breeds allocated, judges, classes and the show secretary's address and telephone number. As schedules are only sent to the previous year's exhibitors, it will be necessary for you to apply for a schedule by post or by telephone. As show dates are always planned well in advance, you will have ample time to study the schedule and choose your classes.

Fill in the entry form taking care that all the details are correct and that the declaration is also signed correctly. Make sure you do not forget to enclose the entry fee. At the same time, write on the cover of your schedule the name of the dog and the classes you have entered. It is easy to forget these important details once the entry has been posted.

THE US SHOW SYSTEM

US All-Breed Shows

In this group system of judging, there are only five regular classes for each breed or variety of breed (see below). Only these classes count towards the required number of points to become a Champion (see below).

After the classes have been judged, the winners compete again in the Winners class, with Winners Dog and Winners Bitch being awarded to the best dog and bitch. Both receive championship points.

Below: *The judge examines a Yorkie on its blue box in the show ring. Boxes can be any colour although they are usually red.*

The best of breed is then selected from all the recorded Champions competing in the show (male and female), plus the Winners Dog and Winners Bitch. From the Winners Dog and Winners Bitch the judge awards Best of Winners. If either Winners Dog or Bitch is selected Best of Breed, it automatically becomes Best of Winners. The breed judging ends with the selection of Best of Opposite Sex to Best of Breed.

The same process takes place in every breed. Then each Best of Breed competes again in its group. Finally, Best in Show is chosen from the winners of all seven groups.

US Breed Specialty Shows

At these shows, the same classes are offered as in the All-Breed Shows, but there is no group showing.

Classes

The classes at Specialty and All-Breed Shows are primarily the same.

Puppy For dogs of 6-12 months of age. The class may be divided into 6-9 months and 9-12 months.

Novice This class is for dogs at least six months of age that have not won a class except Puppy, and have not won more than three times in Novice.

Bred by exhibitor In this class, dogs must be shown by the breeder or co-breeder.

American bred For dogs of six months of age or older bred in the US.

Open For dogs at least six months of age, usually entered by more mature dogs. An imported dog must be entered in this class.

Matches

AKC sanctioned matches for pure-bred dogs competing on an informal basis are given by specialty and all-breed clubs. No Championship points are awarded. These events provide an excellent opportunity for clubs, exhibitors, stewards and those wishing to become judges to gain experience needed for licensed shows. Sometimes a club will give a puppy match, limiting the entry to dogs of 3-12 months of age. This is a good time to socialize your new puppy and gain some show-ring experience.

Obedience and Junior Showmanship classes may be offered at sanctioned or fun matches as well.

Champions

The American Kennel Club awards points towards Championship titles only at AKC Licensed Shows. A dog or bitch must gain 15 points to become a Champion. Championship points are awarded to Winners Dog and Winners Bitch. The number of points awarded at each show will vary according to geographic location and the number of dogs entered. Within these points, two wins must be three points or more; but not more than five points are awarded to any dog. Three, four and five points are considered major wins. Thus, an AKC Champion must have two major wins under two different judges. One and two-point wins are called 'minors'. All Championship show judges are licensed by the AKC.

THE CONTINENTAL SHOW SYSTEM

In Europe, all dog shows are governed by regulations laid down by the FCI (Fédération Cynologique Internationale), with small national differences. Each country also has its own Kennel Club.

Basically there are two main types of show: championship shows and small, informal, fun shows, usually held by breed clubs.

Judging

Judging takes the form of a written critique on each exhibit, graded excellent, very good, good or sufficient. This report is usually written on the spot and passed to the exhibitor. Judging, therefore, can be a lengthy process, but there are far fewer shows in Europe as

well as fewer exhibitions than in either the US or UK.

Classes

Usually, classes are limited to Youth, Open and Championship, although additional classes are allowed. Periodically, there are Brace and Team classes. The Youth class limits exhibits by age, usually 9-24 months.

Awards

Only dogs awarded an excellent grading can be considered for the Best of Sex award. In some countries, the excellent grading is excluded from the Youth class.

Best of Breed is a fairly rare award in Europe. Consequently, there cannot be any group or Best in Show judging. Exhibits deemed to be of outstanding merit over and above the excellent grading may be awarded the CACIB (Certificat d'Aptitude au Championat International de Beauté) or the CAC (Certificat d'Aptitude au Championat). The CACIB can only be awarded at international championship shows.

Above: *The final preparations are always carried out at the show to make sure your Yorkie looks its best. Remember your show kit!*

To become a champion, a dog must be awarded three certificates (CACIB or CAC) under two different judges, with at least a 12-month interval between the first and last certificates. These certificates can be won in any country affiliated to the FCI.

YOUR FIRST SHOW

Preparations

Having decided on the date and venue for your first venture into the show ring, and of course with your dog in tip-top condition, you now have to prepare for the day itself. Keep a special 'show bag' packed with all you will need throughout the day (see below). Remember to feed your Yorkie the evening before the show at the latest. In fact, the earlier you feed on the day before the show the better; it will lessen considerably the chance of the dog being sick during your journey. Also, since it will be a little hungry, the dog will be keener to obey you.

Be prepared for all weathers in a changeable climate — boots, sandals, sweaters and rainwear can all be necessary. The major shows provide benching or cages for all breeds; the benching is for the larger breeds and the cages are provided for all Toy breeds including the Yorkie. These benches and cages are all numbered. For the Championship Shows in the UK, you will have received by post prior to the show your exhibitor's pass combined with your removal order. This numbered pass is your bench and ring number. Take care of the removal order; you will need this when you leave the show. This order is provided to prevent anyone but yourself from leaving the showground with your dog.

In the USA, entry forms must be obtained several weeks in advance. Forms and schedules are available from the show club secretary or from Licensed Show superintendents — details available in *Dog World* magazine or *The American Kennel Gazette*.

At the show site

As soon as you arrive at the show, collect your catalogue; the stand could be a long walk from your bench. Find your cage and give it a quick spray with disinfectant. Make your dog as comfortable as possible with its blanket. Check that the fastenings are safe; you can provide extra safety by tying a lead around the door.

Check your entry in the catalogue. If there are any discrepancies in the details, ie wrong date of birth, class or name, you will need to go to the Show Secretary's tent or stand where they will check your entry form. If it proves to be a printing error, all will be well. If, however, the mistake is your own, you will need to be governed by the Secretary's ruling. Next, find out the time your class will be judged and locate your ring.

Below: *When examining the Yorkshire Terrier, the judge will always divide the coat, as here, to check for 'running' tan.*

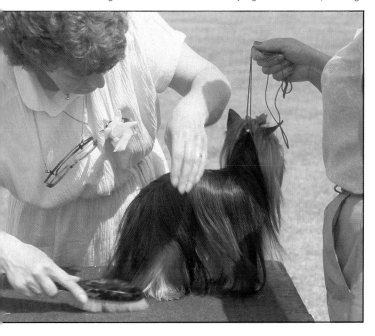

After setting up your grooming table and unpacking your equipment, give your Yorkie a slow and pleasant walk around the showground. This will give it an opportunity to get acclimatized to the noise and atmosphere. Also, it will provide the opportunity to relieve itself if necessary.

Even after the many hours you have spent at home preparing the dog's coat to look its very best, it will still be necessary after the journey to give yourself enough time at the show to give the coat a final brush, ensuring that the topknot, face, moustache, beard and coat are all looking their best.

In the ring

When it is time for your class, walk slowly to your ring. When the class is called enter quietly, collect your ring number which is distributed to all exhibitors by the Steward. This number must be worn in a prominent position where it can easily be seen by the judge and those at the ringside. In the US, an armband bearing your number will be given to you before entering the ring, which should be worn on the left arm. Place your box in line with the other exhibitors leaving enough space for the exhibitor in front and behind you. Now set up your Yorkie to look its very best. Make sure the front and back legs are in the correct position, head well up and back level. The previous training of 'stand and stay' will now be appreciated.

At this point, keep one eye on the judge and one on the dog. After the judge has walked down the line briefly examining all exhibits, his or her attention will then be concentrated on the first exhibit. Now you can relax, praise and again brush the dog until it is your dog's turn to stand on the table for the judge's detailed examination. Never talk to the judge. If asked any questions, answer briefly. These questions are usually in regard to the dog's date

---

Show countdown

Study the schedule
Note the rules and regulations
Make sure both your box and cover are clean and tidy
Pack your show bag
Plan journey to show
Feed your Yorkie early evening before show
Put schedule and passes somewhere near to hand (note benching number on passes)
Make sure you have a towel to keep in the car
Allow ten minutes before departure for dog to relieve itself
Buy catalogue on arrival at show
Check entries and date of birth in catalogue
Find your cage
Place blanket for comfort
Secure cage fastenings with the dog's lead
Offer dog a drink of water or milk
Set up grooming table, etc
Take dog for leisurely walk
Groom your dog
Collect ring number/armband from steward and pin or put on
Place dog on its box
Give final brush to coat
Move dog on your left
Watch and listen to the judge
If placed in the first three, stay until dismissed
Congratulate the winner and thank the judge
Be a good loser

of birth, so do memorize its exact age.

At the conclusion of this examination the judge will instruct you how he or she wishes you to move in order to assess the dog's movement. As mentioned on page 106, this is usually a triangle which enables the judge to see the side movement as well as the front and back. The judge will tell you exactly in which direction he or she wishes this to be executed. With a word of encouragement to your dog, keeping it on the left side on a fairly loose lead, walk smartly with confidence. At the completion of the judge's scrutiny, replace your dog on its box. Now you will be able to make a fuss of your dog and let it relax a little until the judge has seen all the exhibits, when once

again brush and set it up to look its best in readiness for the judge's final selection.

The line-up
Placings of first, second, third, fourth and sometimes fifth are the usual awards. If you have won one of these placings, stay in line until the Steward has given you your card. As the judge's written critique is only given on the first two placings, you may leave the ring. But if placed first or second, wait until the judge has given you permission to leave, then thank the judge, congratulate the exhibitor placed above you and quietly leave the ring.

As already stated, dog shows vary very much in size, but at all these shows, whether large or small, you will be able to talk and learn from other breeders and exhibitors, and in addition enjoy a day out amongst people dedicated to the future and well being of our friend the dog.

Below: *The final line up at Windsor Championship Show, England with the class winner receiving her first prize.*

Appendix

Abbreviations

AI	Artificial insemination
AKC	American Kennel Club
ANKC	Australian National Kennel Club
AOC	Any other colour
AVNSC	Any Variety Not Separately Classified
B	Bitch
BIS	Best in Show
BOB	Best of Breed
BOS	Best Opposite Sex
CAC	Certificat d'aptitude au Championnat de Beauté
CACIB	Certificat d'aptitude au Championnat International de Beauté
CC	Challenge Certificate
CD	Companion Dog (USA)
CDX	Companion Dog Excellent (USA)
Ch	Champion
CKC	Canadian Kennel Club
D	Dog
FCI	Federation Cynologique Internationale
Int Ch	International Champion
JW	Junior Warrant
KC	Kennel Club (UK)
LKA	Ladies Kennel Association (UK)
LOF	Livre des Origines Francais (French Stud Book)
LOSH	Livre Origines St Hubert (Belgian Stud Book)
NAF	Name applied for
Nordic Ch	Nordic Champion
OBCh	Obedience Champion
P	Puppy
Res CC	Reserve Challenge Certificate
S	(Sieger) German Champion
TAF	Transfer applied for
WS	(Weltsieger) World Champion (Germany)

Useful addresses

Kennel clubs

Australia Australian National Kennel Council, Royal Show Grounds, Ascot Vale, Victoria
Belgium Societe Royale Saint-Hubert, Avenue de l'Armee 25, B-1040, Brussels
Canada Canadian Kennel Club, 2150 Bloor Street West, Toronto M6S 1M8, Ontario
France Societie Centrale Canine, 215 Rue St Denis, 75083 Paris, Cedex 02
Germany Verband für das Deutsche Hundewesen (VDH), Postfach 1390, 46 Dortmund
Holland Raad van Beheer op Kynologisch Gebied in Nederland, Emmalaan 16, Amsterdam, Z
Ireland Irish Kennel Club, 23 Earlsfort Terrace, Dublin 2
Italy Ente Nazionale Della Cinofilia Italiana, Viale Premuda, 21 Milan
New Zealand New Zealand Kennel Club, PO Box 19-101, Arow Street, Wellington
Spain Real Sociedad Central de Fomento de las razas en Espana, Los Madrazo 20, Madrid 14
United Kingdom The Kennel Club, 11 Clarges Street, London W1Y 8AB
United States of America American Kennel Club, 51 Madison Avenue, New York, NY 10010; The United Kennel Club Inc, 100 East Kilgore Road, Kalamazoo, MI 49001-5598

Glossary of dog terminology

Affix:	The word used by an owner of a kennel which, when registering a puppy at the Kennel Club, is written in front of the puppy's name to indicate the puppy has been bred by the owner. No one else may use the same word.
Almond eye:	The eye set in an almond-shaped surround.
Angulation:	Angle formed by the bones, mainly the shoulder, forearm, stifle and hock.
Anorchid:	Male animal without testicles.
Anus:	Anterior opening under the tail.
Backline:	Topline of dog from neck to tail.
Balance:	Correctly proportioned animal with correct balance, with one part in regard to another.
Barrel ribs:	Ribs which are so rounded as to interfere with the elbow action.
Bitch:	Female dog.
Brace:	Two dogs of the same breed.
Brace Class:	A class for two exhibits of the same breed owned by one person.
Brisket:	The forepart of the body below the chest between the forelegs.
Brood bitch:	Female used for breeding.
Canine:	Animal of the genus canis which includes dogs, foxes, wolves and jackals.
Canines:	The four large teeth in the front of the mouth, two upper and two lower next to incisors.
Castrate:	To surgically remove the testes of a male.
China eye:	A clear blue eye.
Close coupled:	A dog comparatively short from ribs to pelvis.
Coarse:	Skull heavy in bone, wedge-shaped in muzzle.
Conformation:	The structure and form of the framework of a dog in comparison with the requirements of the Breed Standard.
Cow hocked:	Hocks turned inwards.
Croup:	The back part of the back above the hind legs.

Cryptorchid:	A male dog with neither testicle descended.
Cull:	To eliminate unwanted puppies.
Dam:	Mother of the puppies.
Dew claw:	Extra claw on the inside lower portion of legs.
Dishface:	Nose higher at the end than in the middle or at the stop.
Distemper teeth:	Pitted or discoloured teeth as the result of distemper or other diseases.
Dock:	To shorten the tail by cutting.
Double coat:	Undercoat plus outer longer coat.
Down faced:	Tip of nose below level of stop.
Down in pastern:	Weak or faulty pastern (Metacarpus) ie forelegs bent at pastern.
Drive:	Good thrust of rear quarters.
Dudley nose:	Brown or light brown nose.
Elbow:	The joint at the top of forelegs.
Fall:	Long hair surrounding head.
Femur:	The large heavy bone of the thigh between the pelvis and stifle joint.
Fiddle front:	A crooked front out at elbow, pasterns close and feet turned out.
Forearm:	Front leg between elbow and pastern.
Hackney action:	Front feet lifted high in action.
Hare foot:	A long narrow foot.
Haw:	A third eyelid at the inside corner of the eye.
Heat:	An alternative word for 'season' in bitches.
Height:	Vertical measurements from withers to ground.
Hock:	Lower joint of the hind-legs.
Humerus:	Bone of the upper arm.
In-breeding:	The mating of closely related dogs of the same standard.
Incisors:	Upper and lower front teeth between the canines.
Layback:	The angle of the shoulder blade compared with the vertical.
Leather:	The flap of the ear.
Level bite:	The upper and lower teeth edge to edge.

Yorkshire Terrier clubs
The United Kingdom

Cheshire and North Wales Yorkshire Terrier Society, Mrs P M Grunnill, 16 Brook Lane, Chester CH2 2AP. Tel: Chester 382612; Eastern Counties Yorkshire Terrier Club, Mrs M Millward, Sanbar, Main Road, South Reston, Louth, Lincs. Tel: 0521 50437; Lincoln and Humberside Yorkshire Terrier Club, B R Lees, 109 Nightingale Crescent, Birchwood, Lincoln LN6 0JR. Tel: 0422 694627; Midland Yorkshire Terrier Club, Mrs K Naylor, Holly Cottage, 356 Lichfield Road, Burntwood, Wallsall, Staffs. Tel: Burntwood 71082; Northern Counties Yorkshire Terrier Club, Mrs A Blamires, 482 Bradford Road, Brighouse, West Yorkshire HD6 4ED. Tel: 0484 712678; South Western Yorkshire Terrier Club, Mrs I M Millard, 6 St Andrews Road, Backwell, Bristol BS19 3DL. Tel: Flax Bourton 3689; Ulster Yorkshire Terrier Club, Mrs M Lamont, 65 Old Dundonald Road, Belfast BT16 0XS. Tel: Dundonald 3335; Yorkshire Terrier Club, Mrs B F Whitbread, 13 Weltmore Road, Luton, Beds. Tel: 0582 595329; Yorkshire Terrier Club of Scotland, Mrs M Rillie, 129 St Quivox Road, Prestwick, Ayrshire. Tel: 0292 76072; Yorkshire Terrier Club of South Wales, Mr M D Owens, 29 Rhydyffynon, Pontyates, Llanelli, Dyfed. Tel: 0269 860543.

The United States of America

The Yorkshire Terrier Breed Club of America, Mrs Betty R Dullinger, RFD 2, Box 542, Kezar Falls, ME 04047.

General
The United Kingdom

Groomers Association, 4th Floor, Onslow House, 60-66 Saffron Hill, London EC1N 8QX; National Dog Owners' Association, 39-41 North Road, Islington, London N7; Pet Food Manufacturers' Association, 6 Catherine Street, London WC2B 5JJ.

The United States of America

National Dog Groomers Association, PO Box 101, Clark, Pennsylvania 16113; American Veterinary Medical Association, 930 North Meacham Road, Schaumburg, Illinois 60196.

Bibliography

The Yorkshire Terrier Handbook, Annie Swan, Nicholson & Watson, 1958
The Book of the Dog, Vera Shaw, Cassell & Co Ltd, 1890
Conformation of the Dog, R H Smythe MRCVS, Popular Dogs, 1957
Hutchinson's Dog Encyclopaedia, Hutchinson, 1934
Terriers of the World, Tom Horner, Faber & Faber, 1984
Puppies, Edward C Ash, John Miles Ltd, 1933
Dogs and I, Major Harding Cox, Hutchinson
Our Friend the Dog, Dr Gordon Staples RN, Dean & Son Ltd, 1900
Dogs in Britain, C Hubbard, Macmillan, 1948
The Yorkshire Terrier, Ethel Munday, Popular Dogs, 1958
The Yorkshire Terrier Handbook, Hector F Whitehead, W & G Foyle Ltd, 1961
The Yorkshire Terrier, Its Care and Training, Osman Sameja, K & R Books, 1978

Line breeding:	The mating of related dogs within a line or family to a common ancestor, ie dog to grand-dam or bitch to grand-sire.
Loaded:	Superfluous muscle.
Loin:	Either side of the vertebrae column between the last rib and hip bone.
Maiden:	An unmated bitch, or a dog or bitch that has never won a first prize.
Mate:	The sex act between the dog and bitch.
Molars:	Rear teeth.
Molera:	Incomplete ossification of the skull.
Monorchid:	A male animal with only one testicle in the scrotum.
Muzzle:	The head in front of the eyes, including nose, nostril and jaws.
Occiput:	The rear of the skull.
Oestrum:	The period during which a bitch has her menstrual flow and can be mated.
Out at elbow:	Elbows turning out from the body.
Out at shoulder:	Shoulder blades set too wide, hence just out from the body.
Overshot:	Front teeth (incisors) of the upper jaw overlap and do not touch the teeth of the lower jaw.
Pace:	The left foreleg and left hindleg advance in unison, then the right foreleg and right hindleg, causing a rolling movement.
Pastern:	Foreleg between the carpus and the digits.
Patella:	Knee cap composed of cartilage at the stifle joint.
Pelvis:	Set of bones attached to the end of the spinal column.
Pigeon-toed:	Forefeet inclined inwards.
Prefix:	Usually attached to the dog's name in order to identify it with a particular breeder.
Puppy:	A dog up to 12 months of age.
Quality:	Refinement and finesse.

Quarters:	The two hindlegs.
Register:	To record with the Kennel Club the dog's particulars.
Roach back:	A convex curvature of the back towards the loin.
Scissor bite:	The outside of the lower incisors touches the inner side of the upper incisors.
Second thigh:	The part of the hindquarters from stifle to hock.
Sire:	A dog's male parent.
Snipy:	Muzzle pointed and weak.
Spay:	To surgically remove the ovaries to prevent conception.
Splayed:	Flat feet.
Spring:	The roundness of ribs.
Standard:	A word picture of a breed in type and style.
Sternum:	The brisket or breast bone.
Stifle:	The hindleg above the hock.
Stop:	Indentation between the eyes.
Straight in shoulder:	The shoulder blades straight up and down as against laid back.
Stud:	Male used for breeding.
Stud Book:	A record of pedigree, age, name, breeder and owner of all the recognised breeds.
Sway back:	A sagging back.
Thigh:	Hindquarters from hip to stifle.
Throatiness:	An excess of loose skin under the throat.
Topknot:	Long hair on head.
Topline:	The top outline of the Yorkie in outline.
Undershot:	The front teeth of the lower jaw projecting or overlapping the front teeth of the upper jaw.
Upper arm:	The humerus or bone of the foreleg between shoulder blade and the forearm.
Vent:	The anal opening.
Weaving:	The crossing of the front or hindlegs when in action.
Whelp:	An unweaned puppy.
Whelping:	The act of giving birth.
Wry mouth:	Lower jaw does not line-up with upper jaw.